Christian Unschooling
Questions Answered

edited by Heather Young

Stolen Pixel Books

http://Christianunschooling.com

First edition: August 2018

ISBN: 9781719875868

With thanks to our kids, who encouraged us in our journey to unschooling and radical unschooling, who put up with our mistakes along the way, and who love us anyway.

Table of Contents

Introduction

Who are these people?

The people answering questions throughout the book are all long-time unschoolers who come from a wide range of backgrounds. We all met on the Christian Unschooling Facebook group years ago. Some of us have served as admins of the group and some have contributed articles to the website, while others have just been part of the group because they are so busy with their families and the other stuff going on in their lives. All of us have a wealth of experience working through the process that is unschooling and have successfully unschooled our own children. Many of us now have older teens and young adults who have moved out and moved on with their own lives. At the back of this book you can read our profiles.

What is this book?

The questions themselves are the ones everyone asks. They are the questions that we have answered over and over. We feel that having a variety of answers from many different family types will serve those asking such questions better than just having a single response from a single unschooler, since every family is different.

Why a book?

Over the years people have requested the answers to their questions in book format. Some people just prefer books. We prefer having resources available in as many formats as possible.

How to use this book.

The book is organized in the order that people usually ask the questions. Ideally it would be read front to back but it can also be used in a pinch to look things up.

At the back of this book you will find a list of definitions to various terms thrown around the homeschooling community as well as a list of references that we have found useful.

1. What is Unschooling?

For our family, home education has always been about learning what a child has pursued rather than what an expert recommends. It's about following a child's natural timing rather than a schedule that is deemed appropriate. It's always been about empowering the kids to own their education and to love learning. It's about offering kids the world, and then helping them to get to the parts they choose to explore rather than telling them to follow our path.

It's been about watching them learn without pressure and having faith in the fact that I don't have to control them. It's about learning beside them, every moment of every day, rather than sitting at a table with curriculum between 8:00 and 2:00. It's forgetting that school ever existed anywhere, and just learning through life and organic happenings. It's about letting them move on from something that they decide isn't for them, so as not to miss whatever God has planned for them.

It's about celebrating their learning regardless of where it comes from or whose idea it is. It's about rejoicing in play and childhood fun. It's about recognizing that no day is wasted, whether it's spent watching tv, playing baseball, or reading a book.

Unschooling was what seemed natural compared to duplicating the assembly-line school method at home, though I didn't know that term at first. After a few years I gathered that some call this unschooling, and I've learned that this can be carried over into a family lifestyle rather than just an educational philosophy. It's helped us to let go of panic over how our kids compare to others and worry about how we are representing homeschooling overall. Knowing that there are others who learn like we do is comforting in a way because it helps us stay grounded in our decisions.

We, being Christian, have a second side to our parenting and education. We are accountable to God, so while we are interest-led in topics we also pray out our decisions, listen for God's leading, and trust in His protection for our children. All this differs from homeschooling in that there is no plan, no curriculum, and no expectations or consideration of what others might call accomplishment.

~ Traci Porter

———

Unschooling is living a life without any connection to school at all – as if there were no such thing – because there isn't in our world. It is different from homeschooling because homeschooling is known to mean *school at home*, where learning is blocked off into 'lessons' and 'schoolwork.' We don't even use those terms in our house – they're not forbidden, they just don't fit what we do. How does unschooling work? It works like living life. I know that sounds so simple, but it's the truth. Complications arise when folks feel the need to force or manipulate situations to 'teach' something that can easily be learned naturally if the environment allows. If you forget 'schooling' altogether and just live life as you did the first few months and years of your child's life, learning keeps happening.

~ Dana Tanaro Britt

———

Homeschooling is a lot of different things but mostly it is a system that allows the parents to be in charge of the education and learning under the supervision of the government and with a set program. It makes the parents the teachers as if they were in school in most homes.

Unschooling, on the other hand, allows the parents and children complete freedom in how the children learns based on the *way* they learn. Yes, if the children really do *want* worksheets they can use them and play with them, but they are not made to do it by any outside force; it's up to them. If children want to simply sit and play computer games all day they can because through doing that they are *learning*. (The only game in existence you probably won't learn much from by accident is desert bus and even then you learn how far it is from Tucson, Arizona, to Las Vegas, Nevada.)

Unschooling is letting the world and the parents be the child's teacher rather than the parents and the government being their teacher.

~ Bay Menix (unschooled kid, age 16)

———

Following the interests, strengths, and God-given path of the child rather than what some institution or academia says is essential and appropriate.

Taking everyday experiences, the family dynamic, community and global resources, and passion for life – and calling that an education.

We've had to take a step backwards in our unschooling while here in Korea – family things going on and we needed more structure. But even with using some workbooks and a light schedule (a list of goals for the week), I find that our learning is still radically different from when we were full-on, scheduled, grading homeschoolers.

So the difference I think between homeschooling and unschooling is a lot of trust. Trust in your kids – that they can learn. Trust that you can provide them resources *when* they need them, not before because you fear for their future. Trust in God – that he has given our families every tool we need to grow and be mature in him without having to apply some formula to the education or faith process.

~ Aadel Bussinger

––––––

Unschooling is the non-coercive realization that learning happens best through real life, and that no type of learning is more or less important than another. In practice, it's different from homeschooling in that there aren't educational times vs. non-educational times, nor educational activities vs. non-educational ones. Everything that happens is a space for learning, whether that's reading a book, playing a video game, painting, hiking, writing a story, Skyping with friends, or playing in the bathtub, and none of those things are held up as more valuable than any other. It requires intentional interaction and conversation, and above all trust, but it doesn't require textbooks or workbooks or written proof of subject mastery.

It's fluid, and while it doesn't look the same family to family or from day to day, there are elements that help you recognize it: Freedom. Saying yes whenever possible. Trust. Connection. Peace. And, yes, learning. Day to day, you might overlook it, but when you take a step back, you'll be amazed at all that you and your child have encountered and realized about the world.

~ Joan Concilio

———

Unschooling is a misleading term, in that it has both a negative "un" followed by a reference to school, which of course implies there is some sort of formal, structured transfer of information. There is nothing negative about unschooling, and the only transfer of information is the normal flow from one person to another. Unschooling is life. My children are with me and naturally learn how to live life by living alongside me in the kitchen, at the store, in the laundry room. Of course there is transfer of information going on all the time, because that's what life is. As the more experienced human in the room, there is necessarily a larger flow of information going from me to them; but at the same time they constantly surprise me by the things they know that I know I never taught them … and even more surprising, they teach me something I didn't know.

Unschooling doesn't mean eschewing all formal methods of education on principle. Rather, it means formal education is just one tool with which to approach life. As a grown woman, I know that if I want to learn macramé or differential calculus, I can do so using several methods, from taking a community college class to finding myself a tutor to surfing Youtube for helpful videos. Similarly, if my children want to learn something, we find the right tools to achieve their purpose.

Unschooling also does not mean never influencing a child or suggesting things to her. If I come across information of any sort that I think might interest my husband or another adult friend, I don't hesitate to offer it to them. Similarly, as an adult with considerable experience of the world, I may point out or suggest things to my children, including information about why they might want to do or learn about something that I think might interest them. The catch is, I don't impose it on them as teacher to student, but rather offer it as one human being to another. I know many people fear that such an approach will result in the child refusing all offers, but really the opposite is true. When the child has been constrained his whole life by being forced to accept the what adults want him to do or learn, he will naturally seek to assert his own will by refusing such offers; but a child reared in an atmosphere of trustful respect, in which he has right of refusal, has less to prove by refusing to cooperate. At least, that has been my own experience, and I have four teens who have always been reared in these principles and who are joyful, open, and interested – the exact opposite of what I hear from most other parents about young adults of this age.

~ Carma Paden

————

Unschooling is the process of living and learning without the artificial "school" environment. Unschooling is how infants learn

14

to walk and talk. It's how employees sharpen their skills by reading up in their off-the-job time. It's how "self-made" people become self-made. Unschooling is about pursuing passions and acquiring knowledge in the ways that suit the learner best.

An unschooling lifestyle is a lifestyle that pursues this philosophy by providing children a rich, nurturing environment to explore side by side with parent facilitators who act as partners in learning rather than sole purveyors of knowledge. It is a lifestyle that emphasizes relationship with others and a deeper understanding of self.

~ Mariellen Menix

1a. A Note on Unschooling "Except For"

There's actually a separate name for "partially unschooling." Relaxed/eclectic is its own brand of homeschooling. Because it's so eclectic (drawing from many sources), people tend to swing between gleaning from more traditional homeschoolers and gleaning from unschoolers. I think that actually the majority of homeschoolers fall somewhere in this framework. But as many people reflect when they say "we unschool *except for* math/English/that one subject," relaxed/eclectic tends to rely on traditional academic categories and assumptions, rather than the assumptions that are the driving power behind unschooling.

In order to think "we are unschooling *except for*," which is extremely common in wider homeschooling circles, people have to constrain their definitions of unschooling mostly to how much book work is or isn't used. Going deeper than absorption method allows both unschoolers and eclectic homeschoolers to get a better sense of the underlying principles of unschooling, so they can choose the methods that best suit their own family philosophy, rather than skipping along the surface of method approaches.

So we always answer questions in this group about how to unschool that last tricky subject or two with the answer, "try more deschooling."

We answer this way because in years past we went through a very trying period of attempting to determine why we were investing energy into moderating a group labeled "unschooling" but getting distracted into all kinds of directions that conflicted philosophically with unschooling and that often ended in actual, open conflicts (which was also quite upsetting to witness). That was really crippling to the group's ability to help people understand unschooling clearly and make informed decisions about it. So we chose to specifically focus on helping people understand how to move further towards an unschooling philosophy, not just a curriculum-free method of imparting their educational goals.

So please don't be put off if the answer to "how do I unschool a particular subject?" isn't the answer you were expecting! In unschooling there are no subject categories, so there's no way to give an accurate reply without leaving our philosophical basis — which is the opposite of why we give our time to help.

Deschooling is the years-long process of learning to see those "subjects" in their natural context, in connection with many other aspects of real life and inseparable from them. It lets us see when a type of knowledge is useful, and when it isn't necessary. And it lets us see how that knowledge's form differs from traditional theoretical explanations, as is very common with subjects such as algebra, which permeate life but are incredibly divorced from it when first learning in the basics of formal theory.

It's so much more powerful to learn to see real life and the everyday world, and then pick up formal tools if and when needed to manipulate and interact with the world.

~ Erica C. Maine

2. What Is Radical Unschooling? Is It Biblical/Christian?

As for "is it Christian," the answer is no. It is not Christian, it is neutral, but it is definitely an extension of the example of Christ and how He presented information and in how He treated people of all ages. So, the clearer question is, "Does unschooling fit well with Scripture and the example of Christ?" And the answer is a resounding YES! We were created to learn, and God placed us as part of the whole of His Creation. We can use the whole world and universe and all that is within nature, technology, and humanity to learn all things. We should be constantly in a state of questioning and seeking, and in doing so, we will be able to cover all topics. We should use the example of Christ and treat our children and our spouses with loving kindness, respect, and as equals in worth and consideration in all things.

~ Pam Clark

What is radical unschooling?

 The short answer is relationship first; everything else is gravy.

Long answer: Radical unschooling most often is used to mean an intentional full-life unschooling, rather than of simply education, including character, emotional, and social development. Parents gently guide in the direction that they see God leading their children instead of dictating all aspects of their children's lives. Radical unschooling is NOT unparenting and Christian parents can, and do, do it.

Yes. If you mean, does it work within the context of Biblical understanding; can you be a Christian and unschool. But it does take a paradigm shift if you come from a legalistic or strict background.

I am not going to get into all the Bible verses that support or negate unschooling premises, as scripture can and has been twisted in every direction. Rather I will point out that Christ gently led. Only seldom did He raise His voice or voice His frustration at His followers. He was not weak, He was gentle, kind, and loving. He hurt for His people and for His followers even as He led them. He knew they didn't understand everything He said. He knew they didn't always get it, but rather than berate them, yell at them, or get angry, He continued to love and guide them, showing them gently the right way to go.

Christ's gentle leading has been my own experience with God as well. He guides and loves and shows and allows natural consequences. He doesn't have a huge list of arbitrary rules to show me how to obey but rather asks that I obey out of love, and guides me gently to where I can. Even when I fight against Him all the way, as I did with unschooling and radical unschooling.

He gently led our family first to unschooling, allowing me to fail over and over and damage my relationship with my oldest. Then once we were there He lead us into gentle parenting (which, combined with unschooling, is essentially what radical unschooling is). He helped me rebuild the relationship with my daughter, healing what was broken. He healed the relationship between my children as well, and gave us the blessing of a gentle home.

It isn't always quiet; how can it be with three teens and two adults romping around laughing and playing and being silly together? But it is gentle.

We still have teenagers, hormones still mean crankiness, and still all have rough days but forgiveness comes easily, hearts aren't damaged, and love and joy fill our home where once it was anger and resentment. There is understanding and discussion instead of screaming and fights. There is fun and laughter the majority of the time instead of just occasionally between times of angry parents and crying kids.

~ Heather Young

For us, the transition to radical unschooling has definitely been one that has led us to model our parenting on Christ. So I believe it has aligned with our biblical beliefs smoothly. We are still works in progress, but our efforts have been blessed.

My easiest summary would be to say that radically unschooling is empowering your children to own not only their education but also to own their schedules, relationships, bodies, living environments, etc, so that they know why we live the way we live and can make right choices based on solid reasoning and biblical wisdom rather than just doing what they are told is required. They are still guided and protected; they are expected to respect others; and in our family, they are taught to seek God's direction and will for themselves.

~ Traci Porter

If we parents are Christians and are solid in our own walk with the Lord, all we do should be in alignment with that relationship. Too often, we look to the religiosity of things that many label as "Christian" but really that makes things murky for understanding. *Things* are not Christian, *people* are Christian, so the original question "is unschooling Christian?" hopefully will open people up to looking at the misnomer of it. When we are open to question the little things like that, we can then open ourselves up for the bigger, harder things that might be more uncomfortable to change, but that will benefit our kids, our relationship with our spouses, and our own journey through life.

~ Pam Clark

I personally love and embrace the title of radical unschooler, even with all the misconceptions that abound.

I'm borrowing a bit from something I previously wrote for my blog here: I think that the biggest difference between unschooling and radical unschooling is that generally speaking, the basic term "unschooling" refers only to academics. Most unschoolers will embrace a philosophy of individual life-learning, not following any specific curriculum, letting learning arise from the experiences and interest of the learner, etc, but it doesn't take into account different types of parenting. For example, many people will use the term "unschooling" to define their style of homeschooling … but will still otherwise exert a lot of controlling and punitive rules, regulations, and externally imposed structure on their children. With *radical* unschooling, there is a complete paradigm shift away from a traditional, authoritative, "I'm the parent and I said so" style of parenting to a style of mutual respect and partnership. Radical unschoolers take the trust, freedom, and respect that unschooling gives their children when it comes to learning and extend that freedom to *all* areas of their children's lives. It allows them to honor their own autonomy over their bodies, their sleep, their food, and other aspects of their lives usually completely controlled by parents.

One thing I want to reiterate more than anything else is that radical unschooling is a very *hands-on* style of parenting. I think the biggest misconception people have is that radical unschooling is neglectful, that it's leaving kids to their own devices. It is actually very much the opposite! It is valuing respectful, loving *relationships* over all else. Radical unschoolers guide, listen, model, help, facilitate, and partner with their children. They do *not* control, coerce, punish, or shame.

Do I think radical unschooling is biblical? Goodness, yes. As my understanding of radical unschooling grew, my faith in turn deepened. I think at its heart, radical unschooling is simply extending the same love, grace, and freedom that God gives us and offering it to our children.

~ Jennifer McGrail

———

Grace. Lots and lots of grace, on all sides. Grace from parents to children, grace from children to parents. That combined with love and respect makes an amazing combination and brings much joy.

~ Heather Young

———

I see radical unschooling as three biblical principles:

(1) Live as an example to our children. (2) Be *present* with our children on a daily basis. (3) Disciple and discipline our children (which is not the same as punishment).

"Fix these words of mine in your hearts and minds; tie them as symbols on your hands and bind them on your foreheads. Teach them to your children, talking about them when you sit at home and when you walk along the road, when you lie down and when you get up."

I'd like to answer what radical unschooling is *not*. It is not unparenting or permissive parenting. It is not punitive or controlling. It is not "perfection."

Christian radical unschooling is first and foremost parents who recognize that they are not perfect, but that they desire to cultivate a relationship of mutual respect with their children. They work with their children as human beings and as a family to meet everyone's physical, emotional, and spiritual needs as much as possible. It is about balance, discipleship, relationship, love, gentleness, and grace. All of the things that Jesus spoke much about.

It is also about extending the principles of freedom and grace in learning into the entirety of our lives with our children. We not only give them the freedom to choose what to learn, but the freedom to choose in other areas of their lives. This typically includes a more open and cooperative approach to bedtime, meals, chores, etc.

~ Lilly Walsh

———

I want to add that there is a misconception that we encourage kids to only do what they want, creating irresponsible behaviors. I've observed the opposite to be true because we while we encourage them to pursue things, jobs, relationships, and roles that they want, we also show them that to do so may require hard work, commitment, patience, and endurance of unpleasant times in order to support and achieve these things.

They are fully aware that other groups, communities, families, businesses, etc have rules that may be arbitrary. If they choose to be included by them they should follow their rules. They are responsible and aware that just because we have respected their input here, it is not necessarily how it is done elsewhere. They will have to choose to commit and sit under other more authoritarian environments and I have no doubt that if they choose to they'll be able to behave/work/relate according to those rules.

~ Traci Porter

––––––

While we don't call ourselves anything particular – labels are always distorted by the loudest voices and most often don't truly reflect what we are – for the purposes of this group, we are definitely radical unschoolers. What does that mean for us? It means our connection, our relationship with these kiddos and each other means far more than *anything* else in this world. It means we live life as if school doesn't exist. We learn what we want to, when we want to learn it or when God or life gives it to us to learn from. It means we live life with our kids, together much of the time – we don't leave them behind unless it is their choice, life is for living together. We parent much more gently than we were raised, with a far different approach to 'rules' (we don't even use the word in relation to our home) and in a much more respectful way than is mainstream. At this point in our lives, our kiddos are 21 and almost-19, mainstream parenting says we're done homeschooling, radical unschooling says we're happily sharing life with two young adults who seem to enjoy our company as well as that of their friends. Amid their own lives of jobs and friends, they talk with us, they seek us out – and that is what it's all about.

~ Dana Tanaro Britt

For us it means living alongside our children in a relationship of mutual respect and grace, guiding one another toward being the person God is calling each of us to be. We don't do "rules" but we do principles and guidelines. Our two main guidelines are "Love God with all your heart" and "love your neighbor as yourself." I find that it's hard to beat Jesus when it comes to condensing the spirit of the law.

Is radical unschooling Biblical? I find it to emulate the relationship Christ had with his disciples. I don't know how much more Biblical you can get.

I also want to debunk the "unparenting" myth. I was unparented. I know what unparenting looks like, what it feels like, how it affects a growing human being. I do not unparent my children. I am more involved in my kids' lives than I can even describe. I'm there beside them, guiding them, leading them, acting as friend, adviser, facilitator, counselor, you name it.

~ Mariellen Menix

As a follow-up to the rule breaking, I think you can add that kids will (at least at our house) feel the liberty to walk away from said organization or commitment should they feel it's not biblical or not leading to where they are aiming to go. Hopefully because of the level of respect and responsibility that's modeled in the tough situation they will have seen the "quitting" of a job and how it's done responsibly while still supporting a family. They will have been included in the decision-making process. They will have seen us walk away from a church situation that was unhealthy and seen us make that break responsibly, with prayer and consideration of others. Because they aren't treated as if everything is beyond their level of comprehension, they'll have that experience to fall back on.

~ Traci Porter

That exactly, Traci. That has been our own experience as well. We discuss things with the kids, they know why we left the church we did, they know what our money situation is like, and so on. The respect they receive means they have the tools to handle hard things in life but also to know when and how to stick it out. There is no arbitrary "you have to stick this out"; instead they see real decisions being made and are part of the decisions. They learn a work ethic because they are part of it, they see it, it isn't something that is being imposed, it is a natural part of their lives.

~ Heather Young

2a. Myths and Misconceptions: Is Unschooling Unparenting?

One of the biggest misunderstandings I've found that people have with unschooling, particularly in Christian unschooling, is the question of guidance. People seem to jump to the conclusion that *unschooling* = *unparenting*. Christians assume that if you are unschooling it means you are not guiding your children or "training them up in the way they should go."

So, for the record, let me very clearly state: the parenting philosophy behind unschooling typically involves a *lot* of guidance, y'all!

In my opinion, a large foundation of unschooling is based on parental guidance: being a guide for your child, sharing your experiences and interests, your opinions and your beliefs, while at the same time not forcing a bunch of unnecessary baggage and schedules and lessons on them.

Unschooling is not about watching children make terrible decisions and not saying anything because they're "in charge" of their own life. It's not about watching a two-year-old stand in an ant bed so that they can "life learn" the consequence of that decision. It's not any other ridiculous example of "un"parenting that you can think of.

Now that I've gotten that off my chest, let me share with you an example from our home that shows the balance between guidance and letting kids make their own choices.

Recently, my ten-year-old slept late. Really late. I decided to see how long she would sleep. When noon rolled around, I decided to can the experiment because I really needed to go to the grocery store. She quickly got up when I asked.

Now, ten-year-old does stay up later than her younger brother counterparts. And I totally get why she'd want to. First of all, her dad and I both fight against night-owl-ism. And second, it's the only time she gets alone – absolutely absent from noise and little brothers – to read, write, create, or simply think I asked her why she slept so late that particular day and she told me that she woke up in the middle of the night and couldn't go back to sleep.

The poor girl gets paranoid sometimes in the dark about bugs, or imaginary tapping at her window. or who knows what. So every time she'd almost go back to sleep again, she'd jerk back awake. She didn't finally fall back asleep until sunrise.

Well, that opened up plenty of conversation. I suggested that if she wakes up and the sun is just starting to rise, she could go ahead and get out of bed if she wanted, even if it's before every-one else. She said, "Oh. I didn't know that."

I also talked to her honestly and respectfully about caring for her animals. Since she's chosen to have pets, I reminded her that she's not only responsible for herself, but for them. Just like I'm responsible for her and her brothers. And if I slept till noon too often, they'd probably be pretty lonely and hungry. I did not tell her to go to bed earlier. I did not tell her to get up earlier.

I simply offered her my advice and observations.

Well, that night I noticed that she went to bed a little earlier than normal and the next morning I woke up to the sound of some-one poking around the kitchen. It was ten-year-old — up before me. Which I'm pretty sure has never happened in the history of ever. Even when she was a toddler.

At 6:45 that a.m. she was up, dressed, and packing her backpack. She was taking her dog for an early-morning walk to the park. And packing him breakfast to take with them. Off she went with dog food, treats, and water — before I even had my first cup of coffee.

Why? I believe 100 percent that it was because of my respectful guidance. Because honestly, if I hadn't had that conversation with her, she probably would have stayed up later and slept later again. But, because I try to remember that children are aliens and sometimes need advice about our planet since it's new to them — I offered her some of my observations.

31

Because sometimes I think we forget that kids really don't know things that seem very obvious to us. Like that she could get up really early, when the sky is just lightening up. She didn't know!

So, once again, *unschooling* is not *unparenting*. It's quite the opposite.

~ Jessica Bowman

3. What Is Deschooling?

Who needs it? How long does it last? How do you know you've deschooled enough?

Deschooling for me is the process of healing from the strain of school and schoolish thinking, learning to accept that life is not made up of individual subjects, and that learning happens everywhere, and that out-of-school learning is just as important as in-school learning. Everyone who wants to go the unschooling route needs to deschool – children, their parents, other family members who are directly involved in the unschooled child's day-to-day life. It can last for as little as a few weeks to as long as several years or more. For me, it took about four years to feel that I had really deschooled, and I left school halfway through tenth grade.

I think you know you've deschooled enough when you realize that you're no longer worrying about your children "learning what they need to know," or when the thought of school doesn't send your stress levels spiraling up into the sky. For me, the moment I realized I was deschooled was when I admitted to myself that it might be nice to take some college courses, and the thought didn't make me angry or make me want to cry.

Deschooling was a tough time for me, but it left me feeling confident in my own intelligence and eager to learn things that I'm interested in, and learn them in my own way. It took a long time, but the end result was worth it, so I guess my advice for new unschoolers who are still deschooling is just to have patience. Most children are going to need roughly a month for each year in school, but sensitive children might need twice that, or maybe even more. They'll get there. You, as their parent, will get there, too. You have more than enough time, I promise.

~ Heather Galloway

———

For the kids deschooling meant getting out of the habit of being afraid of anything "educational." At the beginning that meant a lot of "Is this school?!?! Do I have to do it?" And refusing to do things that had any hint of educational value at all. Just like kids in public school not wanting to watch anything that they had ever watched in school because that meant it was "educational" my kids didn't want to do anything they thought was educational, which was extra hard because I loved to point out how educational everything was. This made it was harder on them as they deschooled.

For my oldest, who had the most stress associated with "school," it took a lot longer than it did for the other two who had barely had anything "schooly" (as neither of them ever went to public or private school).

For me, as a former teacher, it took longer to get away from thinking of things in educational terms – but I thought of everything in educational terms and could easily rephrase things into educationese because I was trained to do that.

Because of the type of upbringing I had it took longer for me to get my own fears out of the way, to stop worrying about other people's expectations and focus on who my kids are right now. Not in the future, but how our relationship is at this moment and how I can work on that relationship in, the future, what can I do better, instead of worrying about what things looked like – which is really what most of the education stuff is: what it looks like to outsiders.

Like worrying about whether the kids have bathed or not – we kind of think it has to do with health and cleanliness but really it is usually more about whether other people will think we are neglecting our children. Same goes for educational stuff, because when you look closely and really pay attention there is tons of learning going on, every day, all the time; it just doesn't look like what others might expect it to. And that is the rub.

So deschooling for me was not only getting rid of the school think: since I had always thought outside the box there and was always learning anyway it, for me was more getting rid of the language of education, but even more so it was for me to stop worrying about what outsiders think and trust God that these kids were learning what they needed.

More like pruning out the arbitrary rules than no rules.

~ Heather Young

Deschooling is the process of letting go of the institutional thought processes that go along with school, namely these ideas:

- that life and learning are divided into subjects

- that children must be forced in order to learn the things necessary for life

- that certain interests and academic subjects are more important than others

- that college is a requirement

~ Lilly Walsh

What is deschooling? Deschooling is the process of changing your worldview. When you transition from separating everything into subjects and educational bits vs leisure/hobby/laziness and you start to look at learning in a new light, happening as a natural process of living.

Who needs it? Parents need to deschool the most I think. Kids are born with an innate curiosity, a desire to construct knowledge from their environment. But adults have gone through the rigorous process of school, teaching, and what our culture dictates, so that their ideas about learning, living, and success are colored by that past experience. Adults need to re-evaluate what they value and what they want their kids to value. They need to discover how they really learn themselves. They need to find the joy and curiosity of learning again.

Kids need to deschool if they have previously been to school or have been homeschooled with a curriculum. These kids need to discover joyful learning again. They need to "deprogram" from the idea that kids can only pick up certain skills or knowledge from "on high" – from an authority such as a teacher, book, or lesson. They need to find out what their strengths are, what their passions are, what their beliefs are. They need to have room to think, to question, to explore, to tinker, to quit, to start over, and to *not* do. They need downtime. Downtime is a big thing in deschooling and deprogramming: your mind needs times of lull as well as activity to process everything you are experiencing.

How long does it last? I think only adults really worry about how long it will last – because we want to see some progress or output from the child that tells us that: *yes* this unschooling this is productive. But you have to be careful that you are not evaluating that progress in the old "schoolish" terms. When you can look and see that your kids are happy, that they are thriving (in what they are passionate about), that you hardly ever think about whether they are doing math or history, and when your kids feel free to explore topics and hobbies without you quantifying and qualifying those things in educational terms, I think it is safe to say you are well on your way.

That isn't to say you can never sort your activities into subjects for a transcript or records for the state. The difference is you are seeing learning everywhere, and you are not trying to fit every-thing into an educational box.

> *"Stop thinking schoolishly. Stop acting teacherishly. Stop talking about learning as though it's separate from life."* — Sandra Dodd

How do you know you've deschooled enough? I don't think anyone can determine this except you and your kids. Every family is different. And as you will see, unschoolers are always evaluating and questioning.

In our journey, I've had to deschool many times. Over time, the temptation to break out the workbooks lessons after each deschooling period. I see more benefits of living life without worrying about curriculum.

~ Aadel Bussinger

I don't think there's much I can add to Aadel's answer except this: you're probably about done deschooling when you stop wondering when the deschooling will be over and the unschooling can start.

~ Mariellen Menix

Deschooling for me was a process of changing my thinking and beliefs to understand and embrace that learning need not be measured or graded or quantified. It is a leap of faith to say, "I will not fear that my child is falling behind, that my child needs to know, that other kids are doing x, so my child better do it, too."

Learning happens constantly, and it is not limited to certain "learning times" or "concentrated learning moments." When I let go of the beliefs that society and culture had programmed into me, I realized that each day was spent simply enjoying what is. No, my seven-and-a-half-year-old is not reading yet, but every day, I engage with him in wordplay, and he is showing a ton of signs for reading readiness. But I know my role is not to worry or fuss over it – my role is to provide an environment rich in resources and things which cater to my kids' individualized interests and strengths.

I knew I'd deschooled enough when I no longer compared anything my kids were or were not doing with the school equivalent. It took me about two to three years to entirely let it go and stop even mentally saying, "Oh, he's doing x grade level work!" type of things. Now, I know they are simply doing what is best for them where they are at this stage of life.

~ T. McCloskey

———

It was the process of changing our perspective on what learning looked like. Understanding that there was not a "better" way of learning. That there was not a higher value on books over movies, or curriculum over gaming, or educational over entertaining. That ten hours of reading a classic was not more productive than ten hours on the computer. That passion and interest in something does not equate with addiction. That fear inhibits rational thinking and creates illogical conclusions. That I did not have to see learning taking place in order for learning to be taking place. It just *is*, all the time, and when it is allowed to happen naturally and to the individual's unique wants and needs, it becomes part of the person and not lost to testing or expectations of another.

~ Pam Clark

———

Deschooling is a transition, from a place where we think children will only learn if they are taught, to a place where we know they are learning all the time and it is often invisible to our eyes and doesn't necessarily fit into a school subject box. It is a process, a journey, and it can take quite a long time!

Many people say that it takes about a month of deschooling to recover from every year spent at school, but in my experience it took longer than that, and in some ways it never ends. It is important to remember that the month of deschooling means a month where we actually, fully, completely refrain from any type of schoolish behavior. It is means having a completely school-free month, in both visible work and invisible expectations. So every time we start to panic and make subtle or not-so-subtle comments, or do things that interfere with the deschooling process, it's back to square one and we start counting again. Think of it as being like a board game where you get sent back to start every time you do or think something schooly.

This, for me, helps me to understand why deschooling can take a really long time!

But fortunately, every time we go back to start, we make up that lost progress more quickly, because we have already begun to build a foundation of trust in their learning.

We also need to consider that we parents were in school for many, many years, and often completed tertiary education, too. We are also living in a society that is deeply entrenched in schooling, so we are surrounded by it at every turn. That affects our deschooling, too, and also that of our children, even the ones who have never been to school. Deschooling means getting to a place of trust that our children are totally capable of learning anything and everything that they need or want to learn, without us having to allocate it to a school subject, or tick a box with a sigh of relief that they learned something tangible.

Deschooling requires lots of deep breaths, shifts of focus, and redirection of our nervous energy. When we start to panic, it is a good idea to turn our eyes to ourselves, rather than our children. Instead of focusing on what they are or aren't learning, it is better to focus on having fun, connecting, playing, and exploring, together.

Later, once we are further along on the deschooling path, it will become important for us to also focus on learning within the context of an unschooling life, but during the deschooling phase, too much focus on learning can keep us stuck in "school think" and interfere with our trust that our children are learning all the time, whether they're watching a television show, or playing with Lego, or reading a book, or playing a video game, or seemingly "doing nothing."

Deschooling is a bit like putting blinkers on a horse. We choose to ignore the critics and our inner voice of fear, and we focus on our children, connecting with them in relaxing, fun ways.

~ Karen Bieman

———

Equate the word deschooling with detoxing, and you are most of the way to understanding what it means. School and schoolish thought is pervasive in our society. Most homeschooling and unschooling parents went to school themselves and schoolish thoughts persist in hidden corners, completely unsuspected, waiting to trip up the unwary unschooler.

Once you understand that unschooling means living life as if school and the division of knowledge into subject sets doesn't even exist, and accept that living that way completely is a completely different paradigm for how you connect with and parent your children, then you begin to understand why deschooling – getting the last vestiges of schooly thought out of your head – is important.

Schooly thoughts are judging thoughts: is my child doing, learning, *being* enough? Is my child measuring up to standards that someone else has set? Even if you bite your tongue and don't voice these thoughts aloud to your kids, they can feel the weight of your expectations. Expectations create a burden for kids to live up to – or not – and changes their motivation for doing whatever it is they are doing. When you wonder: is my child doing, learning, *being* enough? then your child begins to wonder: am I doing, learning, *being* enough for my parents? Instead of learning for the joy of it, they learn to please you – essentially, learning for the test, just as in school; except the test has become parental expectations.

~Carma Paden

42

3a. Thoughts on the Deschooling Process

Initially, it can be a very big step to just let go of curriculum. However, after that, there are further steps on the way to fully giving our children's lives over to God's leading.

Relaxed homeschooling is the natural next step when one lets go of the idea of replicating "school at home, only richer/better/ more accepted by the child." The difference between it and un-schooling lies in letting go of school at home, but not (yet) our conceptions of "richer/better," and being content merely with "more accepted by the child," while still trying to live up to school-derived goals such as reading or arithmetic. The following is a compilation of responses by CU moderators explaining ways to get further into the deschooling process.

It can be very tempting to strew according to our interests and goals rather than the child's. For instance, if a child is not accomplishing literacy goals on the parent's schedule, the parent may try strewing materials such as phonics or writing workbooks without voicing an expectation to the child. However, the key is to consider whose interests are being followed and whether respect for both the parent's and the child's comfort levels is being signaled to the child by the parent's example.

If a child is asking, or has shown no desire not to, then strewed material could be a neutral thing that could simply be one new thing. But if a child has stated or indicated they are not wanting to do such a thing, then this could create a stumbling block, or a frustration, and could be a breach of trust because they are not being respected in their choice (possibly need) to wait until they are ready.

Getting to the core of our "why" allows for truly letting go of schoolish thought and avoiding pressure to learn or perform before a child is ready, whether developmentally, emotionally, or physically. Meeting children where they are is important to the principles of unschooling.

Giving tools to children who have already indicated that they do not want something, for whatever reason, and "providing a tool" for them anyway, is not a kindness at that time. It could be excused as strewing in the mind of an adult (though it violates the spirit of unschool strewing), but can have different connotations to the children: the intention of the parent is still to get them reading. Strewing is not intended to be coercive in nature, passively or aggressively.

If a parent refrains from verbally saying "you must learn to read," but sneakily strews learning-to-read materials about the house, the child will feel the weight of those expectations. Not telling kids they have to read (or do whatever) is not necessarily perceived by a child as lack of pressure to read. This is especially true where a child or parent has not deschooled fully. There are still ties to assumptions of expectations whether spoken or not.

Previous schooling (home, public, or private) and schoolish thought are in the adult and in the child. Obedience is tied to those thoughts. Parent gives child something – child is expected to do or learn or perform that something. Perhaps the parent did not verbally tell, ask, or demand, but the internal dialogue remains tied to old patterns and expectations.

Children picking up an offered or quietly strewed item may do so out of desire, curiosity, or perceived obligation. Our assumptions of their reasons may be right, or may be skewed. That is where a hindrance may exist.

~ Pam Clark

———

It pays for us to be aware of when they're still choosing merely the form of knowledge, rather than its real-life function. So a child may pick up a workbook that we call "strewn," and it may or may not be the same thing as academics to the child. A child may gravitate back to a math resource like Khan Academy, which is very academic in style, and it may actually signal that the child hasn't yet felt permission and encouragement to truly release schoolish values – to experience mathematical concepts in the real world.

And I want to reiterate that this is not problematic in itself, it's just an awareness thing of where there's more transformation ahead to completely deschool. This is still schooling at home, just with different cues.

Taking the pressure off enough for kids to resume compliance with schoolish activities without battles is not unschooling. Usually that's all parents actually want from this approach — not to unschool, but to facilitate school-oriented values more gently. That was honestly my only original goal in beginning to unschool too. But fully unschooling has involved a deeper internal transformation of the narratives in my own head and the ones I've gotten the chance to cultivate in my kids' minds and hearts.

~ Erica C. Maine

Particularly with "obedient" children, it never needs to be voiced that something is expected. Something a parent picks out is enough to send the message that "I chose this for you and will be happy if you use it," and suddenly something that seemed innocent to a parent is perceived as a "demand" to a child. It's one of the ways I failed at strewing in the beginning.

~ Mariellen Menix

Pam said: *the internal dialogue remains tied to old patterns and expectations.*

This is huge, and I just want to pull it out of Pam's comments and highlight it. We cannot really see the difference between relaxed homeschooling based on old patterns and expectations and unschooling until we get to a place of transforming the internal dialogues we have about child development and what's important to learn (and how).

This is deeper into the deschooling process, past the "letting go of book work" place, so something to consider and wait on for those just starting out.

Being aware that there are more layers is often more discouraging than helpful without further information. It initially feels like getting told that progress isn't progress. But we're simply talking about a neutral awareness. It is not a success/failure measure.

How can we tell which it is? We can focus on building really deep, no-fault relationships (all things are within Christ's forgiveness and sufficiency) and providing our kids with the language to express their actual perceptions. Asking open-ended questions that suggest words for what they think and feel. Letting them say "yes" or "no" to those words. Going past the invisible limits of "well, if I talk about this I'm opening the door to problems or bad character; this doesn't seem appropriate."

But guess what? They're going to go there in their own minds anyway. The only question is whether we walk along with them and guide them through taboo areas like preference and personality and reactions to the adult world that aren't always grateful and positive.

We are *not* leading our kids into temptation by modeling confessional living. Including "I don't want to learn that." If we're transitioning out of schoolish thinking, that can have the status of a confession. It can feel emotionally risky for both child and parent.

We are very wrongly indoctrinated to view Christianity as ascetic, requiring us to ignore our own needs and our own natural way of getting through life other than to repent of its very existence. But from Genesis to Colossians we see that this is not true to Scripture. In Christ, we are image-bearers of God and can embrace who we uniquely are through His sanctifying power, without fear of cultivating sin. There's great theological justification for embracing the journey, too.

~ Erica C. Maine

———

Unschooling doesn't mean you simply stop telling your kids they have to learn [reading, phonics, math, essay writing, insert your personal fear-of-failure topic], or you teach your kids [insert your fear-of-failure topic] in a new way, or you set books about [insert your fear-of-failure topic] on a table until they get the hint that they have to learn it all.

It also doesn't mean you find [art, computers, music, insert your school topic of greatest comfort level] to be an acceptable alternative and let them learn those.

Unschooling is looking at your kids and saying, "There's a whole world out there, go explore it. Find stuff that intrigues you, stuff you love or stuff that makes you curious, and I'll promise to help you out wherever those interests and passions take you. Go to those intriguing places, whether in a book, through travel, or on a video game. Or, take a look and decide you're not going to after all. You will not be pushed, you will not be judged, you will not be coerced, and this path you choose will be yours."

If you aren't doing that, then you aren't unschooling. Please don't give advice on how to unschool if in reality you're advising people on ways to "sneak in schooly stuff" or "make sure they learn educational things." It's misleading information if someone is trying to unschool, or even if they're just trying to become more relaxed about schoolish things.

We've had new people occasionally feel judged because they're relaxed homeschoolers. We're very clear that relaxed home-schooling is the natural first step along the way. It's chaotic to suddenly throw out absolutely everything you've known. But here's the deal: People have asked to join an unschooling group, and for this to be an unschooling resource in any meaningful sense at all, we can't call it unschooling if it clearly isn't moving beyond school-based values.

These examples of how kids react may not be the case with every child, but we see a lot of it here. Parents come and post about how frustrated they are that their unschooling kids are rejecting the things they offer or are disagreeable and not pursuing anything, when in actuality a lot of what is offered is stuff the parents have handpicked.

Because of this we will often chime in to offer another side to things, rather than just agree that strewing an academic program is a definite solution, because we've seen the opposite results and know that motives, feelings, the child's experiences, and individual personalities can change the outcome greatly.

~ Traci Porter

3b. How Does Deschooling Look Different from Unschooling?

The deschooling period had my oldest avoiding *all* potentially educational stuff: "That sounds educational." She would refuse to talk about anything that might be educational or to watch anything but what we, at that point, considered fluff. She occasionally would request a curriculum at the thrift shop and get it out for herself (we had an English curriculum and a Polish language course and a Japanese language course due to these), and I just told her, "Look, I will buy them, but it is up to you what you do with them," and then never asked again. She used them for a little bit then got bored with them and moved on.

She would force herself to read (she is severely dyslexic) or write in a diary, or whatever, but gradually as we said yes more and stopped demanding things and didn't say *anything* about "educational" things, well, after a while she started telling me about things she had picked up from the fluff tv, or from a video game, or whatever. And then, after a while she stopped asking for things she wouldn't actually use and started showing interest in things she really *would* use and do. She started making friends online and talking to kids (fellow unschoolers) on Skype and just plain living. And it was then that suddenly she started being able to spell, and wanting to write, and doing all the things she had avoided while she figured it out.

The younger two barely needed to deschool at all. I had spent so much time working with oldest (I am a special ed teacher with a severely dyslexic daughter) that the other two were free to go and do and learned to read, and do math, and all the other stuff – all the basics *plus* all the crazy things "they will never pick up on their own." Nowadays they look things up online, learn things organically, and the books are real, interesting books that are actually used instead of "educational" books.

Yes, it does look different. Frankly it is how those of us who have been at it and passed through the deschooling process can recognize those who haven't finished the process yet.

There is a complete paradigm shift from thinking about "school" and "life" as two separate things to thinking about just *life* and knowing that learning is just happening and that God is enough, that He will make sure they have the specifics they need, that He is in control, that He knows them *better* than we do and has an awesome plan that will take all their combined experiences and make them the right person for the future He has for them.

For instance, twenty years ago I *never* would have thought I would be doing what I do now. It isn't what I trained for. It isn't who I thought I would be. Yet, He knew what I needed and led me gradually through each thing I needed in order to have all the experiences necessary for me to be the perfect person for my current job, which fell in my lap at exactly the right time. I never would have even tried to train for it, let alone have known how best to do that. Yet it is an exact match.

Same goes for the group. I never would have imagined leading a group this size. I was a wallflower. I was scared to talk to people. Yet here I am. He knew me, knew my heart, knew my passions, and He put me in this place. Same goes for my husband and the work he does. And we know we can trust Him with our children's futures as well. He knows their hearts, their skills, their passions, their struggles, and He is better able to direct their education than I ever could.

When you are still deschooling you still feel fear – fear of the unknown, fear of what will happen, fear of the future, fear of what people will think. When you move to the other side of it, suddenly the fear is gone. You know they are learning. You see it all the time, regardless of what they are doing. Are they reading a book? Yup, they are learning. Playing a video game? Yup, they are learning. Staring at the clouds? Yup, they are learning. Watching something super fluffy on tv? Yup, they are learning. Dots are being connected, even when they seem to be doing nothing.

It is a huge shift in thinking, and it takes time and effort to get there, to see the learning in everything, to value everything instead of valuing some things over others. It happens gradually for some, and quickly and suddenly for others, but it is a complete shift when it happens. Afterwards you can no longer look at traditional education and see it as having more value than what the kids are doing right now because you realize that there is much more going on internally, even when it seems like they are doing nothing, and that just because it looks like learning is happening in a classroom setting doesn't mean it is.

You do hit a point where you stop questioning, where you stop panicking, where you stop being afraid, where you see value in it all, where you see God can and does use it all. Then you have moved past deschooling into *un*schooling.

Nowadays I have to stop and think when people ask schooly-type questions. I don't even consider what subjects they have covered anymore; I know they are hitting it all, so what does it matter? When people ask what our days look like, I can't give a plan or a schedule, because it is just life and it is joyful and lovely and wonderful. I know for us group admins it is often funny to try to remember, to try to think in "school" terms when someone asks how to put something into educationese. My natural response is, "Why does it matter?" Then I stop and think and have to remember.

~ Heather Young

4. Did Your Spouse Agree with the Decision to Unschool?

If not, is your spouse on board now, and what changed your spouse's position?

My spouse, God love him, entrusts me with all things child-related. For a period of time, he'd make derisive comments like, "They don't even do anything all day." But when I listed what I'd seen them do and what they learned from it, those comments gradually faded away. And the proof has truly been in the pudding! He sees our youngest (never schooled) speaking with a vocabulary and comprehending ideas which would blow most second graders out of the water. He sees their projects and crafts. So while he wasn't on board, he didn't stop us from getting on board.

~ T. McCloskey

No, he wasn't. He didn't understand it at all. It was harder in the early years for him to consider, because like many people he was worried about foundational knowledge. At the time, I kept a blog where I took photos of their projects and categorized things by subjects. Which was hard, because they were usually covering three or four subject areas in any given project.

One of the things that changed and shifted us from eclectic/relaxed more to unschooling was when he began a shift-work job. I absolutely couldn't keep a schedule with him coming and going every two days, alternating days and nights. The reason: he would come home and throw "the schedule" out the window with his desire to spend time having fun with the kids!

So I gave up on that and we rolled with the flow. He's taught them so much hands-on practical math, physics, and chemistry — at an earlier age than a school approach would! He built an ice boat with them in my living room. Taught them vectors, sewing, meteorology, and history with his newly-discovered love of sailboats about six years ago. Taught them carpentry and construction methods by involving them in fixing up our house.

He still sometimes wants them to sit down and do something schoolish, but we don't have the "start-over" problems of full-on deschooling because we haven't been full-on schooled with all the pressure and arbitrary standards that ingrains into a kid's attitude.

~ Erica C. Maine

My husband wasn't initially on board. He was against home-schooling when I started (I am a former teacher). After six weeks weeks in the classroom and listening to my own former teachers repeatedly making fun of my special ed students, I came home and said our children were never setting foot in that school. (I was pregnant with our first – never went back). I spent time researching, praying, and God brought homeschooling (now I know they were unschooling) families into our lives.

Every year my husband would say, we can do this until __ grade (started out first grade, and then gradually moved further and further out), but then they need to go to to school. By the time they reached fourth grade, God had completely changed my husband's heart about elementary and high school. By the time they hit sixth He had changed my husband's heart about the necessity of college and about unschooling. He even wrote about his own experiences as an autodidactic on his blog, then turned it into an autobiographical book.

While he was still in that place, I would journal, take pictures, and keep evidence that they knew that stuff. Pretty soon he stopped panicking. Documenting so he sees what is happening when he is gone really helps for some husbands. Blogging really helped, so did the kids spontaneously sharing all the cool stuff they learned. A little bit of sharing articles, a little bit of talking about what they were doing and learning, a little bit of showing; it all added up to him fully getting it.

~ Heather Young

It was actually my husband's leading to keep our kids home for their education but we unschool because of my style of learning and life. I am the sort who fails miserably at following a curriculum because my kids have needs, interests, and strengths that are not included in some stranger's lesson plans. He understands this so he was supportive of a very relaxed atmosphere of learning. We have always learned organically and he has witnessed it working. He's become even more supportive after meeting other unschoolers and seeing the fruits of their methods, as well as observing our own successes compared to some of the educational struggles of others.

~ Traci Porter

———

My hubs wasn't really on board at first. He was willing to give it a shot ... with caveats. Like "You can unschool everything but history, science, and math. Because they might not learn those any other way." So for a little while we played along with the charade and made half-hearted attempts at doing formal history, science, and math. The first to go was history. My goodness, was that used history textbook boring. It was Texas history, for Pete's sake. We live in Texas. We're passionate about Texas history because we're Texans. This stuff should come alive but instead I watched my kids' eyes glaze over whenever we started talking about Texas. Luckily the hubs noticed too and soon history was, well, history.

Science was the next to bite the dust. We tried doing science experiments we found online. But rather than learn the appointed lessons they were having too much fun watching Peeps joust before exploding all over the microwave. Then they wanted to talk about the smell of burned sugar instead of "so what did we just witness here?" Maybe it was disloyal but the hubs wasn't around to redirect us so I rolled with Peeps jousting and burned sugar. That's what we talked about and learned about instead.

By the time the hubs realized my subversiveness he also saw the fruits of them: kids who could talk about the chemical reactions sugar went through when heated with the expertise of veteran candy makers. Maybe they still don't know Boyle's law but this seems more useful in day-to-day life anyway, right? I'm thinking caramel and creme brulee are probably more common than Boyle's law anyway. Also I'm probably using Boyle's law wrong here because *my* eyes glazed over on the science parts of these science experiments.

Then we were "unschooling everything but math." Truthfully, the hubs never officially gave us the okay to drop the math portion of our day. He just stopped caring or asking so I stopped bothering to tell him little white lies, translating our entirely unschooled days into "what math they encountered today."

Occasionally he still has panic moments. A month or so ago he told me one night that maybe we should have formal handwriting lessons with the kids because their handwriting was illegible. We talked and I argued a bit but instead of putting up a fuss, I just didn't really put any energy into the fight and bided my time. Last week our lefty with the terrible handwriting (who I suspect is slightly dysgraphic) had cause, on her own, to take some notes about a video game she was playing, and after not being able to read her first set of notes, an hour later she spent the time to copy them neatly. It took her four hours to make a fair copy of a single page of notes, but she stuck with it. That night I showed the hubs her fair copy and asked if he still thought she needed "formal" handwriting lessons. I do believe that discussion is over now.

That's basically what I do now whenever the hubs has a panic attack. I don't feed his arguments with any energy whatsoever. I listen to him, I respond on an intellectual level but don't put any feeling into it, and then I wait. Usually if I don't let it get emotional with him he'll let it go long enough for me to deliver a coup de grace that crumbles his wall of panic. But if I get stubborn and tell him he's just panicking or argue unschooling principles it turns into a power struggle between us and I never have the heart to win those.

I'm not suggesting that this would work for everyone. It works with my husband and I because of who *we* are as individuals and how we interact. In the beginning it wouldn't have even worked in our house. He needed to see for himself how it worked and develop his own sense of trust in the philosophy and the genuine curiosity of our kids. During that initial phase he needed me to respect his fears and concerns by making some efforts to assuage them. It did slow down the deschooling process for the kids but it seemed like the lesser evil at the time. And my kids were old enough to understand on an intellectual level that "This isn't ideal but we're going to do it because Dad is still worried and he needs our help to feel comfortable." Because we do put relationship first in our family.

~ Mariellen Menix

———

When we married, we had two kids from my previous marriage and he was open and supportive of beginning to homeschool. We went from school at home (with little desks) that lasted maybe two weeks, and then moved gradually and naturally to unschooling by the time our two youngest were compulsory age. He saw all along that letting go and going with the interests and natural bents of each child was working. Our only regret is that we did not come to unschooling in time for the oldest three to have the benefit.

~ Pam Clark

––––––

Our biggest regret was not unschooling earlier. We really regret not getting radical unschooling earlier. So much of the stuff our oldest deals with would have been assuaged had we caught on sooner.

~ Heather Young

––––––

We too had lots of healing to do when we finally got to radical unschooling.

~ Pam Clark

––––––

My daughter chose to move out at age seventeen because we were so controlling. We had our kids' best interest at heart but, the reality was we limited our trust in them and their choices out of fear. Fear they would make poor choices (based on what believed to be better choices, rather than understanding that different did not equal poor or bad choices), they would not stay in alignment with our beliefs, that they were or would be in rebellion.

Our son was making poor choices that got him in legal troubles. Part of this was probably a bipolar cycle that we did not understand or even know existed, part was his way of taking freedom for his life choices out of tight grip. We fed into each other and his "rebellious ways" were partly of our unintended making. We created an us-against-them scenario that we "needed" to win for the sake of our kids' souls. How arrogant is that kind of thinking?!

Our other son tried out different negative attitudes that he mimicked (as he naturally did not think that way), and with his Asperger's could not grasp how it was not effective for him, but he was feeling out of control due to our controlling and micromanaging.

Once we stepped out from under religious legalism, stepped away from arbitrary rules and limits and really listened to our kids' heart cries and valid complaints against us, we could do different and did. We apologized and then spent a few years living differently and they came to trust the changes in us. They have seen how we treat their younger siblings differently, and they know we are genuine and now we have mutual trust and respect for each other.

~ Pam Clark

And just to punctuate this question in my life, I just posted a link on my timeline about unschooling being scary because it's unconventional but how amazing it is anyway. Five minutes pass and the hubs shares that link on his own timeline, where it will be seen by avidly pro-public school relatives and picked to death. But he's okay with that because he's that passionate about unschooling now.

~ Mariellen Menix

We started out homeschooling on a one-year trial. Hubby was unsure about if that would work and had lots of fears about socialization, learning the basics, keeping up with the school kids, etc. Over the years, he began to accept and even embrace our homeschooling lifestyle.

When I began to learn about unschooling he was unsure. But he trusted me and the kids. It was about that time when he actually made the comment that his whole view of education had changed and he no longer even considered public school an option for us anymore. He really wasn't involved in our homeschooling at that point and so he really just left everything up to me. I brought him ideas and read him little things about the way we learn and letting our kids have more freedom and he tended to see the wisdom in that and agree with me.

Unschooling actually changed the dynamic. Once learning was unchained from the curriculum and schedule, he began to become more involved with the kids and their interests. Learning became a family affair.

He still has doubts sometimes—like about them learning the math they will need. And he worries about me and how stressful it can be for me to stay home and be a single parent fifty percent of the time. So he can get "drill sergeant" (I can say that since he is a soldier) and go back to wanting the kids to be doing "school" for a couple mornings a week – mostly to provide me with some sanity. So we try to work together and come up with solutions. I'm praying that once we get involved with a homeschool group again and have outside activities for the girls to get away from me 24/7 that it will help.

~ Aadel Bussinger

5. When Did You Know Unschooling Was the Right Choice?

How long had you been exploring unschooling at that point? What have been the greatest benefits of seeing it through?

When our oldest daughter was fifteen, I believe, I started looking into unschooling. I purchased Llewellyn's *Teenage Liberation Handbook* and we both read it. She was excited about it (we were *very* relaxed homeschoolers by then) and I was curious and nervous. I did not quite yet understand the principles and was still hung up on the "limits" side of things. We had been homeschooling for over six years by then.

The next year she wanted to attend the public high school for her senior year so she could take marching band and drama. She wanted to walk graduation with her friends, and the school said she had to take three classes (which would be considered full time), so she added Spanish. She had already completed all of our requirements for graduation and could have gotten her diploma then, but she wanted the extra opportunities so we said okay and that ended discussion of unschooling for a while.

I was still trying to wrap my head around it, and had two teen boys with a couple more years of homeschooling ahead of them, but we were just getting to the point we were no longer fearing the "harmful" effects of gaming ... and we let them finish up the few things they were working on for their completion of graduation requirements we had and let them choose how that would happen, and started letting go of the schoolish mindset completely.

Our two younger daughters were in their beginning years of compulsory age by then, and we were able to relax in their early years and had no problems just building relationship with them. They were learning tons and having fun and life was going well and that allowed us to really trust in the process.

We did have two things that veered out of unschooling briefly. I decided that Latin would be a good thing to study. They were not in full agreement, but they went along with it. Partway through that year, a friend's sister went missing and they were needing someone to fill in for her at their Christian Classical School. Since they were doing the same Latin program, I was able to finish the year out for them in the History that accompanied the Latin and my girls joined the class. They also sat in on a humanities class with their friends and enjoyed it. So, the next year we dropped Latin and one decided she wanted to attend the school for the humanities class only. So, she did, and the second semester our other daughter joined in because she wanted to hang out with their friends as well.

Both did extremely well, even though they had never had English or grammar, other than the little bit in the Latin class. They were able to read, discuss, and write papers on books that I had never read, and most likely never will, and do it with relative ease. Their ability to pick up in the middle of coursework and create term papers, take quizzes and tests, and do as well as, or better than, the students who had been in the school longer was the final thing that proved to me that unschooling was effective, and that when given the support and freedom to learn what they wanted, when they wanted, as long as they wanted, and how they wanted ... kids learn.

Part of the process too, was that although they opted to part from unschooling for a brief time, their time at the school was not a burden because it was by their choice. Even the things about it that they were not super thrilled with, they did so with their best efforts, with no prodding to stay on top of their work, because the expectations of the instructor and the rules of the school were part and parcel of their choice. They succeeded or failed by their own efforts and we all knew that any failure would be a learning experience of its own, so no pressure either way.

My girls are now sixteen and fifteen. Both have strengths and weaknesses in different areas. Both are well learned. Both know how to learn what they want and need, how to seek out information, how to research, how to ask questions – and they are so much more comfortable and confident in who they are, even though they do not yet know what path they will be taking once they are ready to go out on their own. There is no rush. One will be done with her compulsory education after next year, and the other the following year. Neither will be expected to leave home soon after, and both will be supported in doing so when they are ready.

Our time with these two has been so pleasant, so less angsty and stress-filled then what we experienced with the older kids. We have been building trusting, respectful, connected friendships throughout the whole of their lives. There will be no need to re-pair relationships with them as we had to with two of the three older kids. We have not lived with the fear and uncertainty re-garding their education because we have seen all along that learning never ceases, and the way and means that they have gathered information through, have all been of equal worth.

We saw glimmers of that with their older siblings, but our fears and biases interfered with being able to offer our older kids the amazing opportunities to choose that which best suited them. When we stopped trying to control and coerce their choices, all of us were able to become better people, individually and to-gether.

~ Pam Clark

————

Unschooling happened for us mostly from the beginning before I knew it was a thing. There wasn't a defining moment to "try unschool as a method," but there was a point where I realized that if I clung to a homeschool process then we would be missing out on so much learning in life. There were so many chances to let them pursue areas of interest that I would have had to say no to, had I been tied up in a curriculum or what I felt needed to be learned.

~ Traci Porter

I got married at twenty and didn't have kids until thirty. In between, I got my degree in elementary education and it was frustration with some things there that drove me to find John Holt's book *Teach Your Own* in the library, years before I even had kids. So my first homeschooling book leaned very unschooly and child-trusting, and made a lot of sense to me.

By the time I finally had kids, I absolutely knew I was going to homeschool, and probably unschool. I had done tons of reading, including homeschool stuff like all of John Holt, all of Raymond and Dorothy Moore, most of John Taylor Gatto, and also parenting and child development stuff like Jean Liedloff's *The Continuum Concept*, Barbara Coloroso's *Kids Are Worth It*, and gentle parenting books like Dr. Sears, so we kind of slipped right into it.

It didn't hurt that my oldest is on the autism spectrum (which we didn't actually know until she was twelve) and I realized quickly that if I tried traditional homeschooling *or* traditional parenting on her, it would be a battle of wills to the death ... probably mine.

So radical unschooling (extending the non-coercive methods of unschooling to parenting practice as well, also known as gentle or respectful parenting) was in focus before her toddler years, in the interest of a peaceful coexistence with my strong-willed-doesn't-begin-to-cover-it daughter.

~ Carma Paden

6. How Do You Respond to Doubters?

Those who give you a hard time, whether family
and extended family and concerned friends? What
about strangers?

Nobody's ever had the guts to just straight-out question to my
face (this is the South, after all, and we are nothing if not polite)
but I get the little roundabout jibes and questions sometimes.
Most of the time I pretend I didn't get it. With closer friends
and relatives I'll explain more and offer resources to learn more
if they're interested and bland reassurances if they're not. Mostly
I let time tell.

It's hard for close friends and relatives to criticize too harshly when the girls are so obviously so much healthier and happier and are clearly learning tons.

~ Mariellen Menix

––––––

I remember one college professor who is important to me who had doubts and questions. We had a long chat about it and in the end, agreed to disagree. We are fortunate enough that we don't live and haven't lived close to family enough that they have had the opportunity to "get all up in our biz," and since "the proof is in the pudding," that's been enough to squash any doubt they may have had. Not that it matters, but it helps that everywhere we go, people – strangers, family, and friends are impressed with our kids. We are definitely fortunate in that although we have several teachers in our family, they actually know all the ins and outs of how we live and they still support us wholeheartedly.

We give strangers a run for their money or flat out don't give in to questioning. I overheard someone grill my oldest on multiplication many years ago and ask her something she didn't readily have an answer for. That one is quick. When she didn't know the answer fast enough, and the questioner bashed homeschooling, she asked for the answer, then she said something like, "Cool! Now I know, and I didn't have to sit in school all day to learn it. Thanks!"

If a stranger, or anyone really, tries to give them a pop quiz, they either say they don't take pop quizzes as they're unschooled, ask the person if they quiz every child they meet, or tell them, "I'll take your quiz if you take mine," then they'll mention something that often scares people away, like the process of encapsulating and tincturing placentas or something.

~ Patrice London

———

For doubters who are willing to listen, I am happy to provide a wealth of resources: books, quotes, websites, blogs, personal analogies, etc. I much prefer working to alleviate a person's fears and concerns than avoiding them. However, I've become rather adept at using "pass the bean dip" strategies (changing the topic) and have gradually phased out spending time around people who refuse to understand or at least mind their own business. Whether it means blocking them from seeing my posts on Facebook or withdrawing from social activities (replacing with something else fun and interesting), it just seems healthier to keep living lives of joy and freedom without feeling condemned or being confronted.

~ T. McCloskey

———

Close friends and family: I respond with all the awesome stuff they are learning (doesn't matter if it would look like school to outsiders). For instance: "Well, my oldest has been spending a lot of time learning about WWI and the cultures and countries involved, as well as spending a lot of time working on higher-level multiplication and division, planning, organizing information, writing stories, and learning Japanese. My middle child has spent hours honing understanding of perspective and spends days reading and writing – the kid is currently full of little-known facts about everything under the sun. My youngest is working specifically on his social skills as well as strategy, planning, organizing information, eye/hand coordination, blah, blah, blah." No one needs to know that this all boils down to watching anime, playing Minecraft, reading novels, playing games with friends online, and drawing. It is all true.

As often as not the kids respond to similar questions and concerns with tidbits of higher-level information that they know the adults questioning won't get.

Even more often I just redirect the conversation, asking about my brother who is still in school, the dog, whatever after a quick, "Oh, they have been really busy with their individual projects."

The same goes for friends and acquaintances. At this point, my kids are older and most adults talking to them pick up quickly that they are intelligent and clearly using their time well as they can converse on most subjects.

If someone is clearly interested then I take into account who is asking and the context. I often direct Christians to the Christian Unschooling website as a resource, as well as to Joyfully Rejoicing, Peter Gray's work, John Holt, and John Taylor Gatto. Also, for those who are interested, I pass along my husband's autobiography about being an autodidact in public school (often forced to ignore his own interests even though at home he was doing things far advanced over what he was allowed to do in school). For those who are just being polite I just say that we focus on their interests, and leave it at that. They don't have a right to any more information than that, if that at all. To especially rude sorts I just say "we homeschool" and walk away or change the topic.

~ Heather Young

———

I usually gauge their interest. I usually just start with "we home-school" and move on from there depending on their questions. If it is a curious mom at the park I might explain that no, I don't sit them down and teach every subject (a lady asked me this recently – homeschooling is rare here in Korea and when done is usually very academically rigid). I explain how we use a lot of different resources, the biggest one being the internet.

I guess I've never had any family or close friends give me a hard time. We are so far away from family that they just don't have any say in how we bring up our kids. We've been homeschooling or unschooling for so long that when I meet new people that is just part of who we are. We might not agree on educational choices but I make a point to not to focus on that. We have friends of all flavors and my kids love knowing people with different experiences. Part of the reason people don't question me is that I really don't let them. I've learned over the years to recognize when someone is genuinely interested in what we do vs. someone who is curious because they want to drill me or my kids or because they want to somehow find fault in our choices. When discussions start going down that road I change the subject or make a statement like, "well this works for our family – not everyone chooses this path and that is okay."

Confidence helps a lot when dealing with people who question or harass you: confidence that what you are doing is best for your family, that you don't have to explain or defend your decisions, that your kids don't need to live up to arbitrary expectations, that unschooling is perfectly legal and leads to maturity in adulthood. People who are new to unschooling can build that confidence by engaging with their kids rather than listening to all the negatives and doubts from the outside. Focus on relationship above your fears of learning and "growing up right."

I think far more often I get irritated with people who know we homeschool or unschool and then reference every person who is thinking about homeschooling to us, expecting me to give advice.

~ Aadel Bussinger

———

Depending on the attitude with which the questions or concerns are presented determines my response. If someone seems to sincerely want to better understand, even if they don't agree, I will go into examples and more details. If they seem to be asking as a more general conversation process, I give surface answers with more homeschool focus over unschooling focus until I can determine if they really want to know more. If they seem more argumentative, I don't go beyond a kind and firm distract and redirect. My time is too valuable to waste it on someone who really does not have an open mind or desire to learn something outside of their comfort zone.

~ Pam Clark

———

I want to add that sometimes if you share all the stuff they *are* learning in response to concerns about them not doing schoolwork, that can relieve a lot of concern. When we travel and visit my in-laws they always love seeing our notebooks and photos of projects and that has helped them become advocates for more relaxed styles of learning. The proof is in the pudding, as they say.

I take screenshots when the kids make something really cool on Minecraft, or when they show me what they have drawn on their tablet. We keep a reading log of all the books they devour in a year. I share what the kids are passionate about (oldest and her cat/dog research, middle and her collecting and preserving flowers and leaves, youngest and his inventions and builds).

~ Aadel Bussinger

I err on the side of cautious truth when talking to people, simply because we live in a state that has many requirements for home-schooling parents. I am very clear that we meet all the regulations of our state, yet we do it in an entirely different method and philosophy than the method mainstream education uses. If it's a complete stranger who is confrontational with me, then I tend to smile and move on. I don't mind what they think of us anyway.

If the concerns come from family or friends I take more time with them, assuming they are civil and not attacking. I might refer them to certain sources if they are concerned that we are making uneducated decisions. I also would reassure them that we follow God's leading above all others'.

What it comes down to, though, is that we see that people learn more efficiently on their own timeline and of their own interests. We've seen the fruits of unschooling in kids who are self-motivated to learn and are not limited by a certain theme of knowledge. In our own home we've seen our children learn things well beyond the grade levels of their friends, simply because we have let their foundation be solid, without cracks caused by hammering in school subjects before they were naturally ready.

There are many reasons to choose a different path for your family. Schools are even unhappy with their paths, so they are carrying the Common Core torch for change, as if it's a solution to become even more regimented. Why then, would we not consider an alternative path of our own rather than following one that has left America behind in many ways?

My husband and I are trying something different, in actual hope that we get different results than what are promised by school rather than worrying that we won't. We don't want what the school offers. We are okay with being in the minority in that, and it certainly isn't an insult to the majority.

~ Traci Porter

I find that I respond best when I am feeling confident and self-assured, but not obnoxious and arrogant; when I remember that I have my journey, and they have theirs; and whilst I don't want them to judge me, they also don't want me to judge them. I don't feel the need to be an unschooling evangelist; I don't need to convince anyone of the merits of this lifestyle.

Often the questioner is genuinely concerned, even though in reality it isn't their business. My confidence and self-assuredness can help to ease their concerns. Sometimes a reference to studies or research can help, too!

If someone is asking questions out of a genuine desire to understand, I tend to give positive little snippets, rather than too much information. Often a short, intriguing answer will have them wanting to know more, whereas a defensive or proselytizing-type comment will cause them to shut down or get defensive themselves.

Another thing I try to do is look for common ground, focusing on things my kids are doing that the questioner is likely to be interested in.

~ Karen Bieman

7. What Were Your Fears About Unschooling?

How did you overcome them?

I decided on unschooling long before I had children, so I was pretty well convinced in my own mind and I don't remember having trouble re-convincing myself. Probably my biggest fear was what other people would think, and having to defend my choices, because I do not do well in confrontational situations. The main way to overcome that fear is just time, I think; at some point the kids are old enough that no one questions your methods anymore, because the results are obvious. Though I did get pretty good at evasive answers that allowed me to quickly change the subject when talking with someone with whom I didn't want to dive into the depths of educational philosophy.

~ Carma Paden

My fears were all about other people. I am a trained teacher and daughter of teachers. I grew up listening to the complaints about parents not doing this or that, poor parenting, lack of educational opportunities or interest in children's education. It was expected that if I did homeschool, of course my kids would do well and be intelligent, and I felt like I had to prove that all the time. I felt like I had to hide the struggles, the tears, the whining, the complaining, the temper tantrums (mom and kids), I felt like I had to force obedience so when we were in public the kids would look good, so I would look good.

And my kids were really good in public. They did great outside the home. It was at home where I felt like a failure, where I wondered what I was doing wrong.

We homeschooled from the beginning with occasional bouts of "sit down everyday and do X" so usually it looked more like a relaxed homeschool environment with no curriculum, just whatever was needed. It was mostly interest based but there were still tears and complaining as we did more Charlotte Mason–style copy work or whatever (mostly just oldest). So even though we were "kind of" unschooling I don't count it as unschooling until we finally left all my baggage behind when my oldest was eight or nine.

God showed me that the younger two were learning naturally while I was trying to force the oldest (I spent all my energy trying to push, trying to help, asking her to read to me, pushing her to read, pushing her to do "educational stuff"). Meanwhile the younger two learned naturally – learned their colors, shapes, letters, numbers, then a little bit of reading here, math there, science, history, all of it. It all happened organically and I never could figure out when or how, it was suddenly there and they could do it.

When I stopped pushing the tears stopped, the tantrums stopped, and my fears diminished. Eventually God pushed me past my fears about what others thought and moved us fully into radical unschooling and again I was amazed. I expected chaos and instead found peace. I expected tantrums and whining and there were none; instead it was polite discourse as we respectfully talked things out, worked things out.

So for us it was God, showing me grace repeatedly and helping me show grace to my kids.

~ Heather Young

I started out unschooling. It just felt right, best and we had so much fun. When my daughter became of school age, I had off-and-on moments of fear that I, or we, weren't doing enough. Learning *had* to be harder than this right? I wondered if it would always work. Maybe there were just some things we would *have* to buckle down and learn traditionally. Each time this happened, I would freak out, buy some sort of curriculum, and we'd get to it. My children were always game; for them, it was like playing school. Thankfully, I can only remember it happening three times. My children were very patient with me and helped me each time. it always astonished me too, that every time I had a freak out session, I found that they'd already learned the concepts in real-life situations. We were wasting time, and I was wasting money.

~ Patrice London

I would probably say fear of judgment from others. We were living with my mother, an ex-teacher, who stated clearly that she was "against homeschooling" (let alone UNschooling!) Living with her during our early months of deschooling was very challenging, because I felt "on show" and was certain she was wondering what on earth we were doing when the kids were spending hours playing on the X box! I felt like I had to prove to her that they were doing and learning cool things.

It was similar with my husband. He was quite skeptical about unschooling for a few years, and was also suffering chronic pain and a major depression, so it was really hard feeling like he was scrutinizing what we were (and weren't!) doing. I would feel very anxious if he asked me direct, heated questions about how they would "ever learn to read" or something like that. It was hard to be calm and not reactive.

I was often afraid of having someone turn up or phone up and find us "doing nothing," or ask the kids what they'd done that day and have a child answer with something like, "Oh, nothing much, just played the X box mostly!"

I felt most relaxed on weekends and after 3:00 on weekdays, because then I didn't feel like we "should be" doing something educational. Funnily enough, that was usually when our best moments of natural learning occurred! And we also had the most fun, because I was more relaxed.

~ Karen Bieman

———

My oldest three started out in a traditional school setting. We started homeschooling when my oldest finished second or third grade (it has been so many years ago I honestly cannot remember). My oldest brought unschooling to my attention at age fifteen after years of relaxed homeschooling. My first fear was regarding how we would be able to figure out graduation at such a late time in her education. So we did not start unschooling with the older ones. We did start shifting our focus though and by the time our youngest two were compulsory age we better understood unschooling principles. My only other uncertainty was if testing would be an issue over time. That concern was put by the wayside soon after as I watched my kids thrive and continue to learn naturally and happily without arbitrary and artificial expectations.

The only thing to fear is fear itself. Let go of it, and trust that learning takes place and trust that if we stop trying to control (even the most minute part of it) our kids, with our partnership, will be well-rounded. Focus on relationship, not a scope and sequence.

~ Pam Clark

My initial fears in regards to homeschooling in general were based on the fact that I knew that I would fail at teaching curriculum. I wanted my kids to explore and follow bunny trails, and I knew that we would be stressed trying to follow someone else's plan for our family. So when I gave up the curriculum idea it became evident to me that I would never fail at unschooling; I was made to do this. It didn't take long for my feelings to change and while I was secure in what we were doing, I wondered how it would work while living in a state that requires fairly detailed reporting. I wasn't willing to be untruthful on my reports so I knew that we needed to learn things that could be translated into the topics that our state requires. I don't know if I would call myself fearful about it but it definitely made me doubtful about how long we could last at doing it.

After three years of successful reporting that feeling has subsided. I not only have been able to report in a truthful and acceptable fashion but since I have to report I also keep track of what exactly is expected at different grade levels. I have found that they have organically covered ninety percent of the topics that would be expected of them at their registered grade levels, and then they've covered countless areas that are well beyond their grades. It's very rare that I have to purposely expose them to something specific in order to meet our state's requirements. I am no longer nervous about reporting, or about the mandatory testing that will start in the higher grades.

~ Traci Porter

I was also very fearful of how to tell people what we were doing, primarily very schooly family. Truthfully I still haven't fully enlightened them. Not that I keep it a secret or lie, I just haven't felt the need to sit them down and dig into specifics with them. I suspect there may still be questions coming because I've been much freer with the word "unschooling," lately and sooner or later someone will probably put that together with sensationalist news coverage. But I'm not worried anymore.

I also worried that I wouldn't "do" enough. Wouldn't strew enough, wouldn't expose them to enough, etc. That has absolutely not been a problem since I completed the paradigm shift into understanding that there aren't "better" or "worse" resources for them to learn from. A day watching Buffy is as valuable as a day dissecting owl pellets. A day of Minecraft and Skyping friends affords as much as a day at the planetarium. So that eliminated that fear.

~ Mariellen Menix

I wasn't sure what high school would be like. I didn't realize how much they'd do for themselves. But to this day, my base fear is always not having all the time and energy four kids need. I chose unschooling because when I tried my husband's suggestion of curriculum, it took even more time and energy. Since I grew up unschooled, for me, this is the easy way. Well, eas*ier*.

~ Erica C. Maine

My fourteen-year-old is the reason we started homeschooling and then unschooling. After fighting him day in, day out, to do schoolwork, there came a point where his determination beat mine. That was the day I was mentally regrouping and watched him happily spend three hours making paper airplanes. He was focused, he stayed on task, but most importantly, I could clearly see learning happening. He was experimenting and observing and applying what he learned to try to improve the next one. The next day, I said, "What do you want to learn?" He quickly replied, "chemistry, electronics, and cooking." I realized when he could choose what he wanted to do, there would no longer be fights. We've been going like that for six years now.

~ T. McCloskey

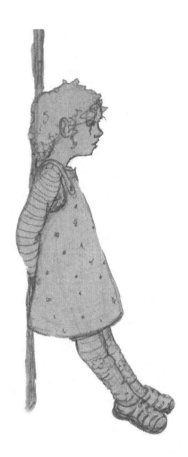

8. Does Radical Unschooling Spoil Children?

I think it is more about letting our kids go out and get want they want rather than limiting them with socially constructed boundaries that we don't think twice about or question whether they really matter in the long run. Unschooling is about a relationship dynamic more than it is about just giving into our kids. We both have a say – and reality kicks in and we can't give our kids everything. They learn through natural boundaries rather than arbitrary ones.

~ Aadel Bussinger

The "spoilt" children that I know have not been spoiled by too much stuff (or too much freedom), but by inconsistent, conditional love and by parents who equate love with stuff. I struggled at first, being in a Christian climate that treats all desire as sinful and teaches that the way to stop someone sinning is to hurt them when they do (and the way to stop children from asking for things is to deny them everything). But at the bottom of it all, I don't believe blessing children causes them to want more, but rather to feel satisfied.

~ Sarah Clark

Also – look up some authors about grace-based parenting; that might help your fears.

~ Aadel Bussinger

I believe that children born into a Christian family know God from their earliest days, and are our brothers and sisters in Christ – so the Biblical way to treat them is as disciples: we walk alongside them, learn and grow with them, and treat them as being responsible for their own selves. Of course if you don't believe that they are our brothers and sisters in Christ, then if anything our responsibility is even greater to lavish love upon them and go the extra mile for them! Radical unschooling and grace-based discipline are for me indistinguishable in the outworking. One may talk about having healthy boundaries, the other may talk about feeling free to say no when you need to – it looks the same in real life. (My favourite grace-based discipline site is Arms of Love Family Fellowship, although she doesn't consider herself an unschooler at all.)

~ Sarah Clark

As others have said, it's not about over-indulging, or even just indulging, the children's every whim. In its simplest definition unschooling is simply learning as life brings you opportunities, and without a forced schedule or curriculum. When you get into radical unschooling, that's when you begin to carry the philosophy over into other aspects of parenting. When you remove "instant unquestioning obedience" as a parenting goal, it opens up so many more options for relating to your child and escorting them gently into the adult world!

As a simple example: I never forced my children to wear a coat when I thought it was cold. If they didn't want one, I would ask them to step outside and check the temperature for themselves. If they still didn't want to wear one, knowing that they might be cold later, I would just bring one along for them. No big deal, no need to turn it into a battle for supremacy on the one hand or an object lesson on the other. Instead, it was a partnership with me (the more experienced partner) being as prepared as possible for what might happen, and the child being given both autonomy and a good opportunity to learn on her own (without being forced) that mom sometimes knows what she's talking about. *And* mom learning that often the kid really isn't cold even if mom is!

Another example: my oldest refused to hold my hand in parking lots or crossing the street. Now she was not a kid who would dash away from me as some will, so I had options. I thought about it and told her she could ride in the cart or put her hand in my pocket, but if she didn't do that then she would need to hold my hand. She usually chose to tuck her hand into my pocket – we never had a problem after that. Later we discovered that she has Asperger syndrome – and at seventeen she *still* doesn't like holding hands! It is a very real sensory issue for her so I'm doubly glad I didn't push it.

~ Carma Paden

9. What Do You Do if Your Child Doesn't Want to Learn?

What advice can you offer newcomers to unschooling who are seeing their kids doing nothing in particular all day every day?

So often there is tons going on internally when they are busy doing things that seem like nothing, seem wasteful. Put it this way – I spend a lot of time working on the computer. I run the Christian Unschooling Facbeook group with the help of my awesome admins, I do website hosting and design, I write, I do bills, I edit and format books, I talk to friends, I work make book covers, I edit my art for print, I read books, I watch movies, I play games. When my grandmother is over she sees me sitting at the computer "doing nothing" because she has no idea what all I am doing. It makes no sense to her.

My grandfather spent hours and hours each day puttering around the garden or in his workshop. Often he was just fussing about and seemed to be doing nothing, yet his garden grew better than anyone I ever met, he would get new ideas for things to create in his workshop randomly – after months of producing nothing he would start making all sorts of wooden toys, or making jewelry from found items, or make a new fountain he has been pondering from scratch..

I often do my best thinking when I am watching mindless tv or playing a video game. I will play an old favorite game or watch something I have seen a hundred times while I am pondering my next painting; I will watch mindless tv or something I have watched over and over while I ponder rearranging the room or solving some other problem. For many creative types it is part of how we process information, how we work things out and come up with solutions. My best paintings take the most internal thinking time. Doodling pictures lead to me getting better and better at drawing. Playing video games, and beating them, gave me a sense of ability – that I *can* solve problems, that I am good enough, that I am capable. I often reread the same books over and over, gaining new insight each read through; same goes for tv. I watch Korean dramas repeatedly – to the outsider it looks like waste of time but I am studying the culture and cultural patterns, the language and how it is used, the language's tones and accents, Hangul (the Korean written alphabet), the different social patterns.

Very often the most amazing things come out of what seems like "doing nothing" to outsiders, and if we respect those around us and recognize that they are not stupid, that there is a reason they are doing what they are doing even if it isn't something we would do, then we give them the freedom to continue or move on, to get what God has for them out of that thing without them feeling they have to stand up for themselves about it.

And when you are new to unschooling, still deschooling, then very often it is scratching an itch, it *is* escapism.

This is what happened to us when we finally had summer vacation, or the weekend. When you go on vacation you want to do what you love to relax. That is what deschooling is, getting all the relaxing in because you are used to having to do it all at once and then go back to the stressful stuff. It takes a while to recognize that the stressful stuff isn't coming back, that you can focus on what you love.

With unschooling we are giving our kids the opportunity to find those things now, in a safe environment, so they aren't suddenly forty and wondering what they did with their lives and suddenly having to go back to school to find what they *really* want to do. (Most of my friends are currently going back to school because only now do they know what they really want to do.)

They get to find it the first time around. They get to test and try and watch and see and learn and grow in a safe environment. They get to watch stupid fluff tv and learn how *not* to have relationships, or pick up little things about history they never would have paid attention to in history class. Maybe they are watching that cartoon over and over because they are fascinated with how the animation works, or how they got the shadows to move like that, or how they got the jokes to be funny, or whatever.

~ Heather Young

———

In addition to echoing Heather, I also want to point out that this is an instance, sometimes, when the *parents* need more deschooling.

When I see someone complain that their child "doesn't want to learn" I wonder if perhaps the kid is happily learning and pursuing their interests and those are interests that the parent doesn't value because they don't fit into the traditional school subject boxes, so to the parent it looks like not learning.

~ Mariellen Menix

———

Well for one, we don't separate our lives into *educational* and *non-educational* because we view everything in life as a learning opportunity. I don't say "educational opportunity" because I don't view unschooling at its very nature as educating. We use things to educate ourselves, but first must come the choice to learn something. And in our house, choosing to play a video game is a choice to learn something.

Here's the thing: unschooling is not hands-off. You don't just say "we are not going to do school anymore, and just do whatever you want." Yes, let your kids choose, but be alongside them. Just because your kids decide to play video games doesn't mean you check out. It means you get to know what they are doing, you ask questions, you be available to answer questions and help them figure things out, you *encourage* their pursuits. You *inform* them that if they love video games they can do other things with that love, such as discuss their favorite games with other kids, make videos, play co-op games, learn how to moderate games, advance in their video game skills.

And I hate that video games always get the bad rap. Because you would want to do the same with any activity your child chooses. If he wants to spend all of his time playing guitar, you would hopefully do the same.

~ Lilly Walsh

———

Exactly, Lilly! And that's why I put "non-educational" in quotes. Again, to me, that harkens back to parents needing more de-schooling because they haven't learned yet to see that there's "educational value" in any activity a learner chooses to pursue in the course of learning a thing, regardless of whether it fits into the schooly box or not.

~ Mariellen Menix

———

My answer would to the question would probably be a return question of "why would you claim to trust them and empower them to educate themselves, but then keep trying to control what they do or learn until it looks like learning to you?"

In our home there is very little separation for "free time." It's all free time. Learning doesn't have to look the way I learned in school, and I certainly hope it isn't all the same outdated and irrelevant subjects. I want my kids to learn about their passions but I really more than anything hope that they find methods of learning that they love so that they are enthusiastic about learning in general.

Stop mistaking things that look schooly for things that are educational. A kid who sits in a very educational classroom listening to very educational lessons can still end up absorbing next to nothing. That same kid could watch a movie and remember every detail about the war that was going on in the story. He could watch *Phineas and Ferb* and add to his vocabulary and science knowledge or be inspired to build something outside of the box. Or he could watch the most mindless cartoon all day, every day, for seventeen days straight, laughing like crazy, being a kid, and appreciating the fact that for once in his life there's no parent or teacher trying to make him learn things he hates by doing things he hates. In fact, you demonstrating that you are empowering him to learn rather than forcing him might be exactly what makes him feel safe to pick up a book someday without worrying about you going back to old ways.

And don't be foolish enough to think that we all are inspired the same way. What seems like stupid tv might inspire him. What seems like a waste of time to one person might be the lightning bolt of ideas for another. I hear people say "Pinterest is such a waste of time." And I look around my house at the DIY projects I've built, knitting and crochet I've done, recipes I've made, homemade products I now use – all from Pinterest ideas and tutorials. I'm a visual learner. It's the way I learn best and if my husband came in and told me I'm only allowed an hour each day to use the internet I'd think, "well, he obviously doesn't want me to learn; he wants to control me." It would not foster a desire to do other things, and it certainly would not empower me.

And last but not least, it takes a long time for someone to deschool. One month of you hovering over him waiting for him to learn is not enough time and is not even really deschooling anyway. I am not a good reference for how long it takes for a parent and a child to forget all about school. (We never truly did school at home so deschooling really wasn't the same for us.) I do know that habits and attitudes in general take a long time to adjust though.

~ Traci Porter

––––––––

The main thing I do in our house is mediate. My husband is as deschooled as he's ever going to get, and his reaction to them doing nothing in particular very much depends on what kind of nothing. Playing a musical instrument all day, okay. Drawing, building things out of scrap lumber, tinkering in the shop, okay. Lying in bed, not helping out, or spending time in front of a screen at the expense of the household's smooth functioning, not okay.

However, because he's also role-modeled an active, inquiring life-style, there's almost always a reason besides "laziness" if one of the kids is being a couch potato. Sometimes emotional, sometimes physical such as PMS or such.

Because I'm home more, I try to be observant and help him understand *why* they're behaving the way they are. I was the child called "lazy" for being non-linear (not naturally adapted to step-by-step tasking), internally rather than externally motivated (who cares about the gold star), and having less physical, more intellectual aptitudes. I've learned I'm not lazy, but environment really, really affects my motivation and even my confidence about exploring and experimenting. In high school, my grades reflected each classroom's social dynamics and approach to study and instruction, not the subject matter itself.

It's a common introvert trait to not feel good about experimenting in front of an audience. Often we need a closed door, such as a video game that's all our own, a sketch pad that's ours, or a computer where we can rough out our creative thoughts without premature critique.

~ Erica C. Maine

———

To echo Erica C. Maine, some outlets have to be private. I have a planner/thinker here. He has intricate plans in his head and he can daydream for hours. Sometimes he is writing stories in his mind, or thinking out blueprints for a Minecraft structure, or contemplating what he wants to do when he grows up. Once I tried to give him a journal to write the stories in and he told me he wasn't at all interested because he doesn't do well with expressing it as words, even though he can picture it all happening like a movie. So now we all have taken to art journaling with captions. Illustrating feelings, thoughts, actions, etc. It's been fun. I also gave him a book of graph paper which he'll use for blueprints now. He likes that. But honestly he has a lot in his mind.

Now to an onlooker he might look lazy, because we can't see what's going on in his mind and he often resists sharing. But, honestly, we as a society could use more thinking and less busyness sometimes so it doesn't disturb me.

~ Traci Porter

———

We started with public school when I was a single mom. When I remarried, we started homeschooling and went from school-at-home to very relaxed with our oldest three. Even with the very relaxed there was still that schoolish thought and expectations at the back of our minds. Our youngest two have always been unschooled and, although schoolish thoughts pop up now and again, we don't give them attention. It truly does interfere with real learning.

If you've never truly let go of separating *educational* from *noneducational*, if you've never tried long-term (like forever) removal of time limitations on gaming or computers or reading or building or *whatever* means your kids are using to learn through, then you can never know the amazing outcomes of it. I'm not referring to natural limitations such as needing to share one computer for a season, but never leaving that season because you purposefully limit access, either by not purchasing more, or not replacing broken items, or setting time limits because you fear they will never do anything else you deem worthwhile, or educational. You'll never see the transformation your child could have through fully trusting in the process, fully trusting that your child will mature, will choose differently or add to what they are doing now.

Every human being has what appears to be "do nothing" moments ... sometimes long stretches of moments. Out of that time for the brain to process, to pull apart, to add to information already there, to mull over, can come greater understanding, new interests, completed goals. Just because we do not see the body move does mean the brain is not working, or the body is not growing and maturing. Assuming a body that is stationary or focused on one thing for a long time is wasting time is a narrow view of life and of human capacity.

No one has to have all things figured out, all things learned, the same things accomplished by age eighteen or twenty-one to become productive, worthwhile adults. Most people do not even come close to knowing what they want to do with their adult lives until they are beyond compulsory school age, beyond college age. Many adults get stuck in whatever they chose (were forced to choose) as teens or young adults, and then they go through their lives stuck in jobs they do not like, careers that are not a good fit for who they are, or will become as they further gain life experience and maturity.

Let go of all preconceived ideas you hold regarding what a "good education" requires, both in subject matter and how it is achieved. Release any dreams you may have created for your child, and let them create their own dreams, follow their own passions, find their own route to what they want to achieve, or what they see as successful. Don't see yourself as their leader to success, but as their partner on the path to their knowing what is success to them. Brings joy to them.

Trust that they will learn what they need to, when they need to. That if given opportunities to go out, do new things, build upon old interests, *they will.* Maybe not when you think they should, but when it really matters to them. Become comfortable with different ways of doing things that were new or that were unavailable when we were young. Be open to all the changes in the world around us, and know that the very activities (even if they seem to be nonactive) they are engrossed in today, may be the very skills that are sought after tomorrow. We live in an amazing day and age that is rapidly changing, and what seemed like improbable science fiction even twenty years ago may be reality within our lifetime and our own children may be at on the cutting edge of amazing things.

~ Pam Clark

I want to echo the ladies above in saying that if you are having those thoughts – my child doesn't want to learn anything, my child spends all the time "zoned out" or doing "non-educational" things – you as a parent need to think through those value judgments. Those statements are placing value on some things and devaluing others. Why? Because those activities are not typically "educational" activities? Life learning is about *all* of life.

I also want to challenge the statement "my child doesn't want to learn" as a fallacy. It's basically the logical argument: My child does X all the time, and X is not educational, therefore my child doesn't have any desire to learn. Or I think my child should be doing X, Y, and Z, but my child in fact does A, B, and C. Therefore my child is not learning.

The problem with that fallacy is that you are defining what is "learning" and excluding real, actual learning that is going on.

~ Aadel Bussinger

10. But What About Socialization?

What is YOUR favorite way to answer the "S" question?

People learn to socialize no matter where they are. If most of their interaction is only with other children exactly the same age, they lose valuable opportunities to interact with others of varying ages in a variety of social situations. They also lose the mentoring that goes along with wiser individuals (not always parents) guiding them.

I've also noticed that outside the classroom setting there is more grace for mistakes or missteps that usually translates to gentle guidance rather than chastisement for error.

~ Rachel Miller

As adults, we socialize with people we have something in common with beyond our birth-date. I find the same for home-schooling and in particular unschooling. Our twelve-year-old daughter *loves* both a local Lego program that's intended for kids a bit younger than she is and an alpaca 4-H club with kids who are mostly older than she is. She thrives when she can converse with adults who share her passion for animals, and she's able to let her interests lead her into deeper and more meaningful relationships than simply picking "the most tolerable of people my age." In a purely practical sense, she actually has more time now to *do* things with friends of all types, because we're not spending hours at night doing this or that middle-school project, and because we can work things like visits to the alpaca farm into our daytime hours!

~ Joan Concilio

Depends who I am talking to and my assessment of their reason for asking. A brief, flippant answer is "the real question is, when do we *stop* socializing long enough to learn anything?" or "hmm, every teacher I ever had told our class that we were NOT there to socialize!"

The more serious answer is that my children are learning to interact with people of all ages and all walks of life in the natural flow of things rather than with a narrow and regimented population segment at prescribed times of the day.

The more lengthy answer delves into the fact that I'm an introvert and school *made* me shy; whereas now I am a mother of three introverts, *none* of whom are shy because they haven't been forced into the unrelenting social onslaught that is school; while my fourth child is an extreme extrovert, born that way and an unstoppable force of nature!

~ Carma Paden

What better way is there for my children to learn healthy social interactions than within a family unit and in the community? My kids know the librarian, the owner of the bread store, and our dairy farmer; they are already active members of society. If you ask me, school stunts social growth by placing kids away from a variety of experiences.

~ Aadel Bussinger

The kids are social, but instead of just with peers their own age they interact with people of all sorts and ages. If you teach a child to love others then they will develop relationships organically rather than becoming friends with whoever is next in the assembly line of school classrooms. They make friends who are their own age and also those who are old enough to be role models which is incredibly valuable. Most people carry only a few good friendships past school, because the majority of relationships tend to be situational. Once removed from the situation of school, we realize we didn't really share much in common with our classmates. Organically developed relationships survive when the situation changes because they are based on people, love, and common interests.

~ Traci Porter

I say: "My kids socialize more and in more healthy ways now that they're free of the dysfunctional social environment of school than they ever did in public school. My youngest even *talks* again now that we homeschool. She had stopped, you know, when she was in public school." Accompanied by a huge smile of gratitude.

~ Mariellen Menix

———

I have only ever actually been asked one time in person; online it comes up constantly. In person, people just need a few minutes with my kids and decide not to ask. The one time was a clueless person who interrupted a conversation between myself, my oldest, and the cashier to ask. The lady was obviously lacking in social skills herself and ignoring the fact that my vivacious child was actively conversing with an adult. I remember the kids pointing out how rude she was when we got to the car.

~ Heather Young

———

Socialization is the insulation of children from one set of influences and the exposure of them to another set of influences. Of course I worry about my children's socialization. I worry thusly:

Placing children in the grade-by-grade public school system insulates them from parents, siblings, older people, younger people, mutually willing mentor-ship, the scheduling flexibility to be of aid to community members in need and receive aid and support from them in turn, the ability to travel and experience different viewpoints, the experience of independent, self-directed learning ... how long should I continue the list? ... and exposes them to a baseline of social intelligence determined by the social skills of same-age peers and the strictures of a highly monitored and controlled institutional environment.

And that's why we homeschool. Because we're worried about our children's socialization. Our society is full of remedial programs to get kids in front of "good role models," to deal with peer pressure, to prevent youth crime, etc, when instead, we can be the change we want to see in our children. I can't choose that for others, but I can choose it for myself.

~ Erica C. Maine

―――

I usually explain that socialization is the ability to function within society. Society is comprised of people from every walk of life – rich, poor, fat, skinny, black, white, old, young, and everything in between. Thus, the very construct of school is a false perception of socialization grouping children by date of manufacture. Spending eight hours a day surrounded by peers with no ability to make choices over one's own fate is not socialization, it's institutionalization. Besides, if I had a nickel for every time I was scolded by teachers saying, "Young lady, this is not a place to socialize! I'd be able to take a really nice cruise. :)

~ T. McCloskey

―――

I've only gotten the question once (from my brother, who doesn't have kids), when my kids were in dance, soccer, going to church every week, playing with the neighbor kids, and we had a friend living with us whose kids are close to my own kids' ages. I listed all that and asked, "How much more socialization do they need?" My brother didn't have much of a reply.

I also had a conversation one time with a homeschool graduate who was telling me how homeschooling gave her the ability to socialize with people of all ages, instead of just her peers. The proof is in the pudding, as they say.

~ Amanda Rodgers

———

And this is the same brother who always encouraged us to spend time alone in solitary, imaginative play. I don't understand what happened to him!

~ Heather Galloway

11. What Preconceived Notion Did You Have About Unschooling?

Lots of things really.

My younger two taught themselves to read while I was busy fussing at my oldest.

My oldest – who hated any form of "learning" thanks to me starting really early with formal homeschooling in a very bossy manner (teacher background with family members all teachers so I had to "prove myself" plus deal with severe learning disabilities of a variety of flavors) – fell in love with history and read every book on the presidents (before Clinton) that she could get her hands on. The girl knows more about the Revolutionary War and the early presidents than most people I know.

All three of my kids can do math in their head in seconds – even my middle child, who, like me, was scared to death of numbers and math (I have severe dyscalculia, written numbers are almost impossible to process mentally) can do all sorts of math without thinking now. My oldest does percentages, fractions, decimals, you name it, without even really thinking about it, in seconds – while I struggle to figure out what a discount is at the store.

~ Heather Young

I never thought my oldest would enjoy writing or math. I remember being fearful to just let go of those two subjects. But now I realize that it wasn't until I finally let go that she could discover how much she enjoyed writing (when it wasn't me pushing her to write) or that she could learn about math (when there wasn't anyone making her feel "behind" or drill facts into her). And it was a shock to me when she asked me to get the *No Fear Shakespeare* books and made a plan to go through them all in the next couple years. It did a mama's heart to hear her tell me that *Romeo and Juliet* wasn't that good and was overrated (my opinion as well).

~ Aadel Bussinger

My oldest, who struggles with severe dyslexia along with other neurological issues, has *learned to spell* and writes happily with her friends! On purpose, because she wants to write stories. She also willingly types with friends and is no longer afraid of messing up. She loves to write and tell stories – which is amazing since when she was younger she really struggled and couldn't spell well enough for the spell checker to even help her. Now she has confidence and is willing to and loves to write.

Also one of the things I never thought would happen is I am no longer a big curmudgeon. I have *joy*. And am *fun*. I used to be super bossy and the "mean parent" because I always felt like I had to enforce the rules. Now my kids talk about how fun I am and enjoy my company. What an amazing blessing!

~ Heather Young

Oh yes – the spelling. It's amazing what chatting online and creating fan fiction will do to a kid's spelling!

My middle child has picked up an interest in botany. What eight-year-old wants to study plants? At a college level? She taught herself to read and has pretty much taught herself up to her level in school (and way beyond in some areas). Complete autodidact. She also loves biographies and I try to find the nice color biography books from the library about people of different races, cultures, and socioeconomic times than us.

~ Aadel Bussinger

That they will be productive, responsible, other-centered, thoughtful human beings without me "training them up" in the traditional way of Christian training and religious upbringing. When we stepped back from all we had been conditioned to believe from the pulpit/Sunday school/church programs/Christian "experts," and instead modeled Christ's love and grace in our daily lives, we saw true desire and relationship in and with our kids. Everything else flows naturally from there

~ Pam Clark

I never imagined I would have a child who was passionate about maths. I never imagined I would spend so much time giggling with my children, or have a nine-year-old who says that she's so glad she doesn't have parents who boss her or threaten her, or that I would be able to say "yes" with a genuine smile to things that I don't actually personally like. I never thought that there would be lollies and sweets in the cupboard and those not be the first things to be eaten.

~ Sarah Clark

Oh yes, Sarah Clark! I *never* imagined my kids would *thank me* for being me and letting them be them. Amazing. Every time we are around bossy grownups they pull me aside after and thank me for changing the way we deal with them and treating them with respect. And they are almost 16, 14, and 12.

And food – I never expected them to turn down junk food and ask for healthy options, or recognize what foods bother them on their own. I guess I thought they were dumb or something. How can they possibly know if I don't tell them. Geez. Sometimes I am shocked at what I used to think.

~ Heather Young

My oldest three read the *Girl Genius* webcomic on the iPod to-gether. Youngest on the other couch, reading a *Girl Genius* print book. Highly social activity. They laugh together, compare obser-vations on the artwork, read out loud here and there.

I hoped they'd be friends, but I never thought it'd be so awesome. Ages 17, 15, 13.

~ Erica C. Maine

––––––––

One that has come up in the past week with my oldest: she came in and told me that Khan Academy has done some updates and it reset her progress then casually added "I never realized math could be so much fun and easy." This girl was public schooled through grade seven. The last two years of public school, her dad or I had to help her with math homework *every night for hours*. And there were tears and fights and shouts of "I just don't get math. It's dumb. Or I'm dumb." When we took her out and immediately started unschooling her, I just assumed she would never approach math again. I wasn't bothered by it. It was just a statement of fact in my head. Two-and-a-half years later, she's voluntarily exploring math on her own. She's still gun-shy of asking me or her dad for help, but that's okay.

My other daughter has made even more profound strides in my book. She was public schooled through grade six, and bullied relentlessly by her classmates from the beginning of that. For the last half of sixth grade she didn't talk. Like at all. Even away from school. She was like a puppy that's been kicked every day until it just sits in a corner and trembles. When she was in a healthy peer group that tried to draw her in she just sat there like a statue. Since pulling her out of school she's pretty much clung to me. She'll be social and have fun and interact but only if I'm around. If I'm not doing something she won't do it either. I have, at times, wondered if she was going to end up forty and still living at home. She's even said she hates birthdays and growing up because it means someday she'll have to leave me.

Guess what she did last week? She went to a friend's house (a friend with four kids!) and hung out and baked while I was at the doctor. Totally without me. All day. And talked and had fun. She even ignored the safety of the adult women for a while and went to curry the horses with their teenage son.

~ Mariellen Menix

———

Like Heather said, there have been lots of things. But one that I've been thinking about recently is in the area of chores. We've been radical unschoolers for years and years, and it still gives me such a tickle every time I see one of the boys deciding to bring out the recycling bin, for instance. Not because they were told to, not because they were even asked to, but just because they noticed it was full.

~ Jennifer McGrail

12. What Happened When You Lifted Screen Time Restrictions?

I never thought my kids would love math because all I ever knew was the math that was forced in school. We have never "taught" them math, and I am continually amazed at how much they pick up, understand, and love. My oldest loves playing math games. He is always pointing out to me his calculations.

I also never thought my kids would love things like geography and history. They love both. My oldest taught himself many of the states when he was very into a state puzzle that he was given for Christmas one year. They also love watching videos with us and learning about history. I hated history in school because I thought it was boring. I am finally finding a love of history and having so much fun learning it casually with my kids. It is so re-freshing to see them enjoy learning about the past and other parts of the world without being told what they must learn.

I have also been pleasantly surprised at lifting screen-time re-striction and have see positive effects of doing so. I was very leery of trying it in the beginning. The difference now is not re-ally that they watch less. We as a whole family spend a lot of time on screens for entertainment, for connection with friends and family, and for learning. What I do notice is that they freely walk away from electronics, where as before they were glued to the screens because they knew it would be "taken away" soon.

And despite my fears of "they will never want to do anything else," it's just not true. They have been begging me for days to go play in the snow. It has been too cold until yesterday when the two older boys ventured out into the backyard. They spend equal time going off to build forts, play with toys, get out a board game to play.

But we have also been very blessed by the non-stressful screen time. By lifting the restrictions, my kids spend lots of time teaching each other through the use of "screens." They learn to work together to beat levels, find their favorite Youtube videos. They bond and we bond as a family by a mutual love of certain TV series, of being interested in a topic and researching it together, Skyping with long-distance family, meeting new friends online, watching very silly or very interesting Youtube videos on the big TV as a family.

I could go on and on about how no limits to screen time has blessed our family.

~ Lilly Walsh

For us it took a while. Months. I realize though that I may have made it worse because even though I let them play, I'd still be voicing irritation and I'd blame or threaten to take the games away, etc. God pointed something out to me though. What I wanted to fix was sinful and disrespectful behaviors (lying and saying they did something when they didn't, ignoring people's request to spend time with them, etc). So instead of saying "I'm going to get rid of Minecraft if you keep up this behavior" as if Minecraft were the cause, I started to explain sin, selfishness, relationships, people's feelings etc. Every time someone would speak to my son and he would zone out, I would go over and ask him to pause it ASAP and taught him how to stop a game when company came, etc. I helped him remember that he wouldn't hurt a game's feelings by pausing it, or even just saving at the next level and turning it off. We talked about Skype friends and how they would understand that when his cousins were there he'd want to sign off and play with them. I once even pitched a fit when someone interrupted me, to demonstrate what that behavior looked like.

We also stressed that if you're hurting someone's feelings then chances are you're doing something wrong. Either you are being rude, or not communicating that you need some alone time, or not using your tools (pause button, dvr, etc) well. There are ways to use screens while still being kind and well-mannered. We also explained that if you say "hold on one minute and then I'll come," then you need to *come* in that one minute ... not forty-five minutes later. (We all procrastinate).

One example I think of was I asked him how his aunt would feel if she took time to come for coffee and I played on my phone the whole time. That, he understood. He actually pointed out to me that I do it to him sometimes. So we agreed that screens should be put down or turned off in favor of company.

~ Traci Porter

———

For those who still prefer to be online, either they have nothing more interesting being offered *or* this is a passion and they are getting a lot out of it! If a friend comes over, do they play together or one plays and the other watches? My older boys used to do this and the cooperative help on the games was phenomenal! Sometimes they played at our house, sometimes at a friends. This was their favorite thing to do for months on end. Then one day they discovered parkour and we would not see them for hours at a time.

~ Pam Clark

———

We also have "human time" every day. It was our way of making sure that we play with each other during the day because some were feeling neglected.

~ Traci Porter

———

I agree that finding a way to connect is a good thing. Figuring out what is that "thing" that can bring you together is worth the time and effort.

~ Pam Clark

12a. A Note on Technology

Technology, and giving our children unlimited access to it, plays a big role in their learning. It has provided wonderful opportunities for our family to connect and strengthen our relationships.

Before I share some of our favorite resources, I wanted to share a bit about the common "objections" to technology and the word *screen time*.

You'll often see articles in the media and recommendations from professional groups encouraging parents to severely limit the amount of time children spend in front of screens. It's been stated that television and gaming contribute to obesity and a sedentary life, foster violence, and are addictive. The biggest issue with these studies is that they are done on public school students. Each day a student spends up to an hour sitting on the bus, another seven hours sitting in class, another hour sitting on the bus home, another thirty minutes to four hours (depending on the grade) sitting doing homework – that's over forty hours a week.

You have a person already living a sedentary lifestyle. Any additional activity spent sitting is only exacerbating the situation – by the way, this would also include interests like reading, knitting, playing an instrument, etc. As homeschoolers, this does not have to apply to you.

In regards to fostering violence, the media latched onto a perceived correlation between violent acts (again, schooled students) and the commonality that perpetrators played violent video games. However, when actual data was reviewed, researchers at Villanova University and Rutgers University concluded:

> *"Annual trends in video game sales for the past thirty-three years were unrelated to violent crime both concurrently and up to four years later. Unexpectedly, monthly sales of video games were related to concurrent decreases in aggravated assaults and were unrelated to homicides. Searches for violent video game walk-throughs and guides were also related to decreases in aggravated assaults and homicides two months later. Finally, homicides tended to decrease in the months following the release of popular M-rated violent video games.*
>
> *Finding that a young man who committed a violent crime also played a popular video game, such as Call of Duty, Halo, or Grand Theft Auto, is as pointless as pointing out that the*

criminal also wore socks."

Another common objection to television and gaming is that they are addictive. Clinically speaking, addiction is defined as:

> *"a primary, chronic disease of brain reward, motivation, memory, and related circuitry. Dysfunction in these circuits leads to characteristic biological, psychological, social and spiritual manifestations. This is reflected in an individual pathologically pursuing reward and/or relief by substance use and other behaviors."*

Do I believe that someone can become addicted to video games or television? Absolutely. Just as someone can become addicted to food, exercise, or sex – all of which also play a meaningful part in our lives. For nearly forty years, since the Rat Park studies of the late 1970s, researchers and medical professionals have repeatedly found that addictions often disappeared when the environment of the addicted was positively changed. The drugs, alcohol, and video games are a means to producing a euphoric effect combating a perceived miserable situation. Remember how I detailed earlier that more than forty hours a week of a schooled student's life is dictated by someone else? Who wouldn't want to escape? The solution to or prevention of addiction is not to forbid or limit your child from video games and television (or food, or exercise), it's to facilitate an environment and foster a relationship they don't feel the need to try to escape from.

I would also like to address the phrase *screen time* because it is loaded with a lot of assumptions and negative connotation. Our family doesn't use it in our everyday vernacular, but I've referred to it here, because of its prevalence. When our children are reading, coloring, or writing, we don't refer to it as *paper time*. We don't negatively lump any other multitude of activities into one category based on commonality. It's dismissive to a child's interest and keeps you, as parents, from gaining a better understanding of the specific activity and your child.

Okay, let's get started with some resources our family enjoys.

Books! Yes, books and technology go together. Many public libraries have teamed up with Overdrive to bring you books in digital or audio format and streaming video that you can borrow for free. Since they are loaned digitally, they are automatically returned at the end of the lending period and there are never any fees. To get started, you'll need a library card and a device to read your books on: computer, tablet, e-reader, or smartphone. Download the Overdrive app for free. Some books may only be available in Kindle format. Amazon also provides a free app that you can download to your device.

If you have a child who is having difficulty learning to read (for whatever reason) or has a hard time retaining read information, consider checking out audiobooks to listen to while reading the words. I have several friends who have children with dyslexia who found this to be incredibly beneficial to their children.

Another great resource is Khan Academy. While this can be used as a more traditional "schooling" approach with assignments and tracking, our family has chosen to use it as a reference source. A parent account and linked student accounts can be created and videos can be watched via an internet browser, an app, or on YouTube. Families living in states that require more documentation may find the logging by Khan Academy useful.

Several websites, including Coursera, edX, MIT Open Course Ware, and more offer college courses (both live and pre-recorded) for free online. Some even offer the ability to earn a certificate. Taking classes "real time" can give your child an idea of the demands and rigor of college classes without worrying about their permanent record. Taking a previously published course allows students to work through material at their own speed and convenience.

Just because a resource isn't labeled *educational* doesn't mean that our children aren't learning from it. The people who design or write video games, program apps, television shows, and costumes for movie characters all bring their own knowledge and experiences to their efforts. Not to mention the additional research designers and contributors do as the project unfolds.

Themes might include a historical period, literary characters, or geography. Many games inherently involve math concepts like algebra, geometry, and finances. While these "bunny trails of learning" may appear to be superficial, they can translate into a deeper study sometime in the future. A favorite movie like *Lord of the Rings* may foster an interest in costuming which may translate into sewing and designing. A TV show like *House* may parlay into an interest about anatomy or a desire to learn CPR. A game like *Dota 2* that references characters from *A Midsummer Night's Dream* can expand to an interest in Shakespeare. An app like *Scribblenauts* encourages players to be a little wild in their answers which helps expand their vocabulary. Even the frustration that a game doesn't have the functionality or features they desire might become the impetus to learn coding.

Consider buying or borrowing a copy of a film or TV show that includes a Special Features section. One of our most treasured investments in film is a 12-disk Special Extended Edition of *The Lord of the Rings*. Each movie is so long it's broken into two DVDs and has two DVDs of additional material that include sections like: what it took to translate a book from the written medium to writing a script that would translate to the screen, storyboards, artwork, scouting locations, designing and building Middle Earth, composing and recording the musical score, casting, filming, interviews with the actors, and the numerous obstacles the entire teams had to overcome.

One of our daughter's favorite movies is *How to Train Your Dragon*. She watched the movie and the TV show endlessly. The main character, Hiccup, is an artist and designer of all types of contraptions. Our daughter created a sketchbook from scratch and began copying his sketches and adding more of her own. She designed and built dragons from the story, including turning our game room couch into a dragon that she could ride with a head, saddle, and tail. Last spring, she researched online to find more information about the upcoming sequel. She also found an online game called *School of Dragons* which, in addition to allowing her to expand on her interest in the theme, introduces topics and information on Viking history, farming, scientific method, commerce, and following directions to complete missions.

Scribblenauts Remix was a favorite app for quite a while (and there are several different apps as well as Wii U and DS games in the genre). This game is a fun way to encourage spelling and reading. When we first downloaded it, our son was already fairly comfortable reading all that is presented, while using his creativity challenged him to spell new words. Our daughter was an emerging reader and needed help understanding some of Maxwell's requests. Even though my husband and I are happy to spell whatever word is called out to us, she would often sit down with her *Big Book of Words* to look up the spelling of what she's trying to give Maxwell. If a player misspells a word, *Scribblenauts* suggests words they possibly meant, allowing players to self-correct. Additionally, some words have multiple meanings and the game will ask which the player would like to give Maxwell. For example, if they type "chicken" the game will ask "chicken (bird)" or "chicken (food)." Selecting the bird will place a living chicken to roam Maxwell's world. Selecting food will place a cooked leg for Maxwell to eat. Probably one of the best features of the game is the flexibility of the "right" answer. For example: in Word 1, Level 1, Maxwell needs to cut down a tree and grab the star from the top. In addition to "saw," you can give Maxwell a drill and he can cut it down, you can give him a bomb to blow it up (don't stand too close or Maxwell will be blown up too!), you can place a beaver next to the tree that will chew it down, etc. We often go back to previous levels to find new and creative ways to complete tasks. One of our daughter's favorite thing to provide Maxwell with: "flying socks."

Another fun, incredibly simple, yet open-ended app is *Rory's Story Cubes*. This is a digital version of a hugely popular dice game. Nine cubes with a picture on each of six sides equals fifty-four pictures and millions of combinations. Pictures include representations of an eye, beetle, house, star, footprint, apple, scales, bee, keyhole, fountain, bridge. The user rolls the cubes either by tapping the roll button or shaking the device. Then we begin with the ever-popular *once upon a time* and we're off creating fanciful stories. The cubes can be easily manipulated and rearranged on the screen so that you can formulate your story. There's a lock function so that cubes won't be disturbed as storytelling commences. Tales can be as complicated or simplistic as desired.

Use it to encourage writing skills as well. Simplistic pictures allow for a wide range of interpretation; for example one time our son decided the "arrow" was a spear for hunting, while our daughter used it to determine the direction her character is traveling. They have been known to each build a story from the same set of blocks just to see what the other comes up with. Individual or group thinking is encouraged. The whole family has sat around concocting stories. Leave the cubes as they land and let each person take a turn adding to the story with the next cube. For even more ideas, visit the *Rory's Story Cube* link Ways to Play.

Beyond simple games on PBS Kids, Minecraft was probably our first significant exploration of the world of online gaming. While it seems incredibly simplistic in terms of graphics, we have found the tangents to be complex and unlimited. For those of you who are unfamiliar, it would be easily described a virtual Lego. In creative mode, an endless supply of blocks allows users to create buildings, farms, tools, weapons, and dig mines. In survival mode they would have to start from scratch to acquire the items. For example: they would cut down a tree, turn the wood into a shovel or pick-ax and then use that to mine in the ground to uncover stone or coal. They could combine the wood with coal and build a torch to see at night. And on from there. If you don't have any idea of what I'm talking about, I highly recommend Minecraft Dad's tutorials on YouTube. They are family-friendly and a great overview of the basics of Minecraft. Like any other open-ended game the possibilities for learning are exponential. One of the first Minecraft servers our kids played on was a "peaceful" server comprised of other Christian home-schoolers and unschoolers. It fostered a respectful atmosphere where each player had a protected plot of land as well as community areas suggested or built by players including a post office, stores, police station, and a public pool. It was interesting to see the kids come together at one point to decide that their world needed a government. They determined a mayor and other political and government positions, held elections, had term limits, enacted laws, etc. That's not to say that "peaceful" is the only way to learn. There are many public and private servers based on books, movies, cartoons, and other video games with various levels of cooperative or competitive objectives and obstacles.

Minecraft was also our children's first experience with "chat" functions. It helped improve their reading and spelling as well as their ability to communicate effectively and succinctly.

Steam is another popular platform for gaming in our home. Steam is different from platforms like the Wii or PlayStation in that it is based on the PC or Mac. It is also free, which significantly reduces the upfront financial investment (provided you already own a computer), in contrast to the $350 you'll need to shell out for an X Box One. One of the things that I appreciate about Steam is the wide variety of co-op multiplayer games. Our daughter, in particular, doesn't like playing competitively. So, games like *Battleblock Theater*, *Don't Starve Together*, and *Portal2* allow players to work together to complete tasks. Not only do the games themselves provide opportunity to problem solve, but working together as a team sharpens our interpersonal and communication skills. Several obstacles can be overcome in more than one way, which encourages players to approach it in numerous ways. Do they want to save time, save resources, or build a foundation for a future hurdle?

Skills our son has gained from Steam are understanding concepts like investments, bartering, budgeting, and saving. Steam has a wishlist option where players can add games they are interested in purchasing. They have sales several times a year and notify users when a wishlist game goes on sale. There is also a market-place where users can trade, sell, and buy items that they earn in games or extra content that may have come as a bonus during a purchase. For example, during the winter sale, our son purchased a four-pack of a game at a significant discount. The game was originally $10 per copy. He purchased the four-pack for $10 to-tal, for an individual cost of $2.50 per copy. He kept one for himself and gifted copies to two other friends. He kept the re-maining copy in his inventory, until recently when he bartered it to someone in trade for an item worth $8.

YouTube is another wonderful resource. You can find lessons for playing an instrument, instructions on how to load the bob-bin on your sewing machine when you lost the manual, walk-throughs of video games, geographical phenomenon like watch-ing a volcano erupt, building instructions for the garden, and pretty much any other topic you can think of. To link YouTube further to gaming and how you can learn from gaming, we've enjoyed the GameTheorists and Gaijin Goomba channels, where reviewers further examine historical, cultural, social, as well as controversies within games (language/content warning). Many kids like to set up their own video logs. Creating an account, es-tablishing their own channel, talking about safety, and following through with producing and posting content is a wonderful learning experience.

I wanted to mention e-mail. So many of these online resources rely on e-mail to create a login and to track individual prefer-ences or achievements. I strongly recommend creating an e-mail address for each of your children. Shared family accounts make it difficult, sometimes impossible, to play together. Since my husband and I already had gmail accounts, it was easiest for us to create e-mail for our children through Google. Because they don't (by their own choice) check their e-mail, we chose to have their incoming e-mails automatically forwarded to ours so that we didn't have to constantly logout of our e-mail to login to theirs.

Most online logins will ask how old the person is. Some people use their children's actual birthdays under the assumption that it will provide protection for them (especially if they're under 13). Unfortunately, we've found this actually makes things more difficult and removes our ability to make parental judgments as to whether or not something is appropriate or useful for a particular child. For instance, Skype will not let you create an account if the birth-date provided shows that the child is under thirteen. Our entire family sharing one account is a logistical nightmare (especially since we've been known to Skype each other within the house). So, we use the parent's birthdays and they each get their own account.

If you are new to the concepts, you may be asking yourself, "How on earth do you know all this?" It's easy: we play *with* our kids. We have accounts on Minecraft, Steam, Roblox, Skype, Facebook, Twitter, Instagram, YouTube, School of Dragons, Khan Academy, Coursera, etc. This has the dual advantage that we have a better understanding of what and how they are learning because we're witnessing and experiencing it ourselves and it's an opportunity to strengthen our relationship. I don't know everything about every game or every episode. I certainly don't play or watch as much as our children, but when I watch or play with them, I learn the lingo: gaming terms such as DLC, NPC,

FPS, or the names of their favorite YouTube channel, or characters in a favorite TV show. Later when I can't play with them, but they're telling me about a new game, new YouTube upload, or a recent episode while I'm cooking dinner, I can fully participate in the conversation because I know what they're talking about.

I want to ask you not to get hung up on the specific shows, movies, apps, or games that I've shared. These are just examples from our family. These same learning trails and connection opportunities can be found anywhere and in any medium. Enjoy discovering them with your children.

~ Rachel Miller

13. How Do You Talk About Unschooling?

Sometimes, it seems like the dirty little secret of the home-schooling universe.

For a lot of different reasons, many of them entirely valid, there aren't too many unschoolers who go beyond the proverbial whispers of "We don't exactly use a curriculum…" and "Don't tell anyone, but we don't take tests!" when asked about their style by friends and family members.

Those of us who blog here at CU are obviously pretty open – but we hear from readers and like-minded friends all the time, "I just can't talk about this without there being problems."

Now, I'm weird. I not only talk about unschooling to, oh, anyone who'll listen, I'm also a columnist for my hometown newspaper – and I've shared about our philosophy in print and online there as well!

The thing is, there are certainly pitfalls. Do I worry sometimes that we're being judged and found wanting? Absolutely. In fact, sometimes I think my openness is the problem, not my un-schooliness.

When Carma shared our short answers to the "socialization" question last week, it made me realize that sometimes I can be a little OVER-enthusiastic. So where's the balance? How do we talk about unschooling, and especially how do we respond to questions, in a constructive and positive way?

1. Be concise.

Says the woman who writes the longest blog posts in history. The thing is, when a friend asks you about your homeschooling approach, *especially* if she doesn't homeschool, she doesn't need a treatise on your views on all systems of education from preschool to grad school, your journey from Charlotte Mason and the boxes of curriculum you sold at a yard sale when you realized you wanted to be free of it all.

I've found that succinct but friendly answers will often open the door to future conversations – but long ones can turn listeners off.

2. Don't be defensive.

Oh, wait, I'm guilty of this one too. Sometimes, people ARE asking questions because they want to find fault. That's the sad truth. Sometimes, we think they want to find fault, but they really don't!

Either way, the only part you can control is your response. A smile and a warm answer, even to someone who is purposely looking to be critical, can help defuse a tense situation. And in the case where the asker was legitimately just curious, you've avoided creating a "you vs. them" approach!

3. Speak for your family only.

On my blog, on Facebook, and in conversations with friends in real life, I have to be real careful not to paint unschooling with a broad brush. "Oh, unschooling is awesome! You don't have to ..." is my former and uber-enthusiastic conversation piece. Then there's, "You really should try doing a more relaxed style for ..."

I am no authority on much. I can speak for my family. I can't speak for what would work well from my friends, their friends, my blog readers, or my cousin's neighbor's family. I can't even speak for what works for other friends who call themselves un-schoolers – except to spread the word about their blogs and let them tell their own stories.

My conversations got a ton better when I answered questions about what I'm doing with what *I'm* doing. Imagine that.

4. Stick to a few specific examples.

They say a picture is worth a thousand words, right? I can talk all day about our approach and philosophy – or I can give one (again, succinct!) example of how a situation played out in our lives.

People connect with stories.

Here's a great example of this: on Facebook, a large group I'm part of asked, "How do you fit in your lessons with holiday ap-pointments? Before? After? Work on the weekends instead?"

My knee-jerk answer was to go on a long "thing" about how we learn the same at all times of the year, based on our interests, find the "learning" in the things we're doing anyway, relax and let the season happen, blah blah blah. That's probably not going to make me any friends, especially since the question was phrased in a way that showed me that most of the group members fol-low a more traditional school format.

Instead, I simply gave an example of how great it was today to have an impromptu conversation with my daughter, Sarah, about the chemistry and mathematics involved in making our Christmas gingerbread cookies. I also mentioned that we spend a lot of time reading together before bed, and the great thing is that we can do that even while traveling.

Honestly, I "said" the same thing. I got across the idea that we're informal, and that we learn through our life activities, and that we don't try to fit a defined schedule of coursework into our days. But I did it in a way that even people who might never un-school can relate to.

I'm still a work in progress. But I'm consciously trying to make my conversations about unschooling not only open, but con-structive!

~ Joan Concilio

_____

14. What Is Strewing?

How do you go about strewing? Do you have any advice for new unschoolers as to how to strew with confidence and without pressure?

Strewing is so incredibly simple it feels strange to me to even have a word for it. It's sharing or making available things that you think might interest one or more of your kids. The secret, as with sharing anything, is not to get too involved in if or how another person chooses to receive what we've shared. Do we get upset with our friends for not reading this great new book we discovered? Do we get disappointed when our husbands aren't interested in the myriad patterns and designs of Jamberry nail shields? Usually we understand that not everybody will be interested in everything. That is, for me, the crux of strewing.

~ Mariellen Menix

The bathroom – I put books that may otherwise go unnoticed but are interesting if they get picked up on our small book shelf in the bathroom. I also keep an open Bible in there. In the past we have had a world map shower curtain, posters of random interest in the bathroom, on walls in hallway, as place-mats on table.

When I find something cool online I share it with my kids via whatever online means I am currently using to communicate with my kids.

With littles, think about how when you clean a room they suddenly want to do all sorts of things in it. That is the key to strewing with littles. Clean a spot, set some cool stuff out, and see what they use.

Also strew on online streaming services like Netflix or set up a playlist of cool stuff on Youtube for them. You can add things to favorites or shout, "Hey, come here, look at this cool thing I just found!" We do that a lot. We all share interesting tidbits throughout the day. Kids share with us, we share with them.

~ Heather Young

———

A favorite tip from my mother-in-law: for younger ones, have storage boxes and rotate the strewings of educational toys and games seasonally. Might be every six months or every three, whatever works for your house. It freshens up the continually loved things while keeping the space tidier and keeping the kids from getting overwhelmed by "stuff organization" and tidying up.

Currently, with teens, I try to do a couple of book purchases every few months. Amazon, second-hand store, whatever.

We, too, do a lot of "hey, check out this YouTube video!"

~ Erica C. Maine

Having a place that is safe for older kids to have their stuff without worrying about younger ones breaking, destroying, or eating things.

Having a few places you always keep neat and randomly set out new, interesting things is good. With littles just putting a toy they haven't played with for a while opens up whole new worlds.

Also, not getting upset when they mix and match toys. That is as important as putting out new things. Mine used to come up with all sorts of new games and things using old parts. We just had a bin where the things that got misplaced would go so we could find them when we went to use the game.

When I was small my bed had a bunk-bed top and I used it for playing with my doll house and other small things I couldn't play with on the floor (brother was four years younger).

~ Heather Young

My best tip on strewing – it's not the same as spewing. Less is often more. And go for quality over quantity also.

A lot of new unschoolers make the mistake of either stepping back and becoming uninvolved in their child's learning journey, or they see strewing as a way to get kids to do schooly, educational subjects. Neither extreme is conducive to unschooling.

Left alone, especially if they have previously been to school or homeschooled in a rigid way, kids don't have the resources to see the wideness of the world and the joy of learning naturally from it. Strewing is a way to enhance their experience. It's not a manipulative tool.

~ Aadel Bussinger

———

We do a lot of different things here, but whatever I do I have to do on a minuscule budget. The public library is a great resource for us. It allows the kids to pick out what interests them and it allows me to surprise them with things too. I also like it because it can be an outing. I have littles right now, but I'm slowly transitioning into the point where my son and daughter (8 and 5) will be skipping story hour and just spending some time in quiet corners reading while I still take the youngest for the read aloud.

I also like to "naturally strew" by walking around our old town pointing out old architecture, through cemeteries and remarking on headstones, park visits, walks in the woods, etc. I always carry my camera so they can take a picture of something in case they want to Google it later, a field guide for identification, their nature journals in case they want to draw or write about something they find, etc.

Netflix is always resourceful. I also keep Pinterest boards with stuff that I think will interest them. In the local college town where I take my son for violin class there is a book stand outside the library where you can take free books and any donation goes towards the local humane society. Each week I check it out and will grab books or puzzles from it and leave them in baskets next to our recliners. Some of the books are just one-time reads that I'll re-donate. (I'm stocking our classics quite nicely too.)

In our family, strewing works one of two ways. Sometimes I'll look for things that seem to fit their current lines of interest and I'll come right out and offer them. Other times I just find new things that are great or that I think might draw their attention and I'll just expose them in baskets, on a bulletin board, via Pinterest, etc. The important thing is that I don't put emotional merit on whether or not they seem interested. I just give and let go of it, without pressure. When they were loving Lewis and Clark I was beginning to feel like they would *never* move on to a new topic. Eventually they took hold on the Civil War and I was never so excited for fresh interests.

They will sometimes immediately like something I strew. Other things will catch their eyes six months later. Even other things never have been interesting to them. It's not insulting to me, and it's not important in the grand scheme of things. I am so excited to see how the pieces of this educational puzzle fit together as they get older.

Some specific ways that I've had strewing success: I keep magnetic poetry on the fridge. It's taught them a lot about sentence structure. The toddlers have always had foam letters in the bathtub. We have a short (coffee-table height) table that is painted with chalkboard paint. I will write math-y puzzles or riddles on it, fill-in-the-blank limericks or mad libs, factoids, etc. They sometimes will attack them trying to find a solution. Other times they'll take a while but they seem to like the variety. Our kitchen table has a basket as part of the centerpiece where we keep story cubes, card games, etc, and we will often end up playing after dinner. I put quotes and scripture on chalkboards around the house. (I love words and would do this regardless but it's an added bonus that they read them.) I try to include whatever their Bible verse was in church that week. On our DVR I'll record interesting shows and leave them for watching at leisure. I keep some bins of things that I'll pull out and leave on a table on occasion: miscellaneous building supplies, art supplies, old clocks, etc; things that they can pull apart, put together or create with. Right now we've had craft supplies on our dining table for four days (much to hubby's dismay). They will randomly sit down and make a valentine for someone, make a puppet, make some origami swans, etc.

~ Traci Porter

––––––––

A great example of strewing happened this week. Our twelve-year-old's computer died. We offered to pay for the base computer kit and he could save to add to it. My husband asked advice of his readers. I took the advice and researched options that fit our price range, then compiled those into a Google drive document which I shared with hubby and son. Son and I sat down, discussed options, the advice, what he wanted, what he needed. He made final decision but before this didn't feel he had enough info or confidence to research alone. After this he helped build his new computer and was able to, once I gave him the site we planned to order the stuff he was saving for from, research on his own to choose which keyboard he wanted. Next time he will know where to look on his own and how to research options.

~ Heather Young

Another thing that some people overlook is the blank spaces that are windows. We have been known to use dry erase markers to make maps, trace the trees in the yard beyond, play hangman, trace our bodies for silhouettes, etc. I've also torn apart outdated calendars with famous paintings, landmarks, etc, on them and tape the pictures on the windows. Once we drew a huge timeline on one, and for fun we drew a map of Middle Earth. Just beware, use a tape that comes off easily. I know that another way to expose my kids to great new stuff is to encourage the grandparents to give them magazine subscriptions, either snail mail (they like to get the mail from the box) or digital.

~ Traci Porter

We bought a lot of books at the thrift store. Old vintage science books are awesome. And our veterans' thrift store even sold magazines for ten cents – we got a lot of fun ideas from old magazines.

~ Aadel Bussinger

Another good thing to do is for them to be friendly with older people. I can still remember so many stories that my elderly neighbor used to tell me. She was so excited to share stuff she'd talk for hours. And I didn't mind because she baked good cookies!

~ Traci Porter

And one of the best stewing I have found is people. My oldest loves art and drawing and connecting her with artists and art curators has been encouragement for her. Going to family book discussion, talking with farmers about animals, setting up a monthly meeting with our elderly neighbor (who was a Christian but liberal in her political beliefs and they would discuss world events and she would read the same books as the girls to have something to talk about).

~ Aadel Bussinger

Our library has audio books (most do), like the books that come with a cassette tape or CD to read along with. I think they can be a great learning tool.

They also lend out these *huge* puppets of various animals, people, etc that are fun to take and act out silly history scenes with. (I'm just always a little paranoid about keeping them in great condition while we have them.)

~ Traci Porter

How do I strew for my kids? I hand them things from the mailbox with the words, "Here, would you like to look at this?" I e-mail them links to articles, websites, or other internet resources I think might interest them. I find things at the store (like flarp putty) and leave them on their desks. I surprise them with new shower curtains that I think will pique their interest. I toss interesting books into the book rack by their toilet. I say, "Hey, I'm going to watch this movie that I think you'll like. Do you want to watch with me?" I leave a puzzle or game on the table and wait to see who goes for it first.

~ Mariellen Menix

———

For absolute newbies, recovering from school or school at home, or just controlling parenting, my suggestion would be to start with strewing things in line with what they are already interested in, then expanding and enhancing that. It's too easy early on for us to strew things we "think they should learn" or stuff that is too schooly, and it is easy for the kids to then get a bit suspicious of our strewing after that. Once they start to trust that we have their best interests at heart, and really do want to support them in what they're interested in, I think strewing new and different stuff works better. I guess it depends how much recovery, detoxing and deschooling there is to be done.

~ Karen Bieman

———

It really does change and adjust as you learn to trust each other. I remember Pam commenting at one point about how she wouldn't strew *Life of Fred* language arts because she knew her kids would not appreciate it – they would assume the wrong intent if she did and they wouldn't like it so why would she strew it. Same goes here. There are certain things I will not strew even if I would like them to read or watch or whatever – that is stuff they need to discover on their own, with no sense that I put it in their way because it will make them feel I am manipulating them, or attempting to, regardless of my intent. And it depends on the person. If I message my oldest certain things she would be upset instead of take it the way I intended, partly due to our history and partly due to who she is. I could send the same to my middle child who would be all over it.

So know your kids, put relationship first, start out with their interests and gradually, slowly start putting things they may not be interested in but which they may decide is interesting ... but still, know your kids. Relationship first.

~ Heather Young

14a. Strewing – What Could Possibly Go Wrong?

During my deschooling phase (which took far longer than it needed to), as I journeyed towards really getting unschooling, I struggled with one main question:

How much should I do? How much should I suggest and offer ideas and activities?

I couldn't get my head around it. I was learning to trust that my children would learn from living life, I was learning to set them free ... but I wasn't sure how much to "let them be," and how much to suggest ideas for activities and outings, etc. How active should my role be? When I heard about the concept of "strewing" I realized I had found my answer! And I went at it with gusto!

Unsuccessful Strewing

I would take them to the library ... and get frustrated if they only wanted to borrow DVDs instead of "all those interesting books."

We would end up coming home with piles of borrowed material anyway – mostly chosen by me, of course. Many of the books would never be opened ... and I would comment (of course) on what a "waste" it was.

I would leave an interesting (to me) book opened on the coffee table and it would often stay untouched ... and I would sigh.

I would suggest an outing or activity and the response would often be, "Ah, no, I'm not really interested," or "Maybe" ... and my heart would sink. I had been hoping for something more like, "Yeah, Mum, that's an *awesome* idea! You're the *best*! You come up with *awesome* ideas!"

For ages I was completely unaware that when they responded without the enthusiasm I'd hoped for, I would subconsciously do my "magical maneuver": a super-subtle eye-roll that was invisible to me, but very visible to them. They could sense it somehow, and hear my almost-silent sigh. They knew.

They knew I was not happy with their response. They knew I was offering something I *really* wanted them to want to do.

If they didn't respond with boundless enthusiasm, I took it personally. I judged their choice as less than what I had suggested. I really thought they should do it, or at least *want* to do it.

Expectations and "Should-ness"

But "should-ness" is soul sapping. Maybe their lacklustre enthusiasm was because of the attachment I unknowingly had to the activity, or perhaps they honestly just weren't interested.

Either way, my subtle response was not so subtle in its damaging effect on their deschooling journey. And it was damaging to me: my trust would decrease and my frustration would increase. I had this picture in my head of what our life outside of school should look like, and their responses to my occasional suggestions weren't in keeping with my idea!

I was way too attached to my desired outcome: their enthusiastic response. So when it wasn't forthcoming, I was disappointed. And they knew it.

What I was doing wasn't really strewing at all: it was *product placement*! With a very clear expectation that they would "purchase" what I was selling.

Their responses to my early strewing attempts became my teacher (I have learned so much from my kids!). I realised:

The things I was placing around the house, or suggesting we do, definitely had strings attached – put there by me.

They were also often too "schooly," especially for those early deschooling days. I was still thinking in school subjects, so was mostly offering things that would tick an imaginary educational

147

box for me and a "boring" box for them: perhaps a history documentary or a science experiment etc. The evidence that I overdid that kind of strewing is that my two grown unschoolers who were my "unschooling guinea-pigs" still mention "history documentaries" and "science experiments" from time to time with a not-so-subtle rolling of their eyes – accompanied by a knowing smile, as we look back on those days from a much better place now!

Beyond School Subjects

My "strewing" during our deschooling phase looked a bit more like stuffing things down their throats, expecting them to lick their lips and ask for more! To their credit (aren't kids amazing?), they knew that they needed more freedom than that and so they did not lap up my lashings of schooly strewing. Their resistance drove me a little crazy at the time, but looking back I can see they were still deschooling, needing to detox from everything "school," and find their happy joyful place. Looking back, I am so very thankful they felt free to say no.

It took conscious effort to let go of my attachments and expectations, and to learn to love and honour what mattered to *them*, not me. Instead of suggesting that we read a historical novel together, or subscribe to an "educational" magazine, I would have been better off

- Playing the video game they loved, with them!

- Going to the beach and exploring the rock-pools – without the "subtle" science lesson!

- Cooking delicious food because it tasted great and was fun to make – not because it was an opportunity to do maths!

- Going to the movies to see what they wanted to watch, not the one I thought might involve learning something – they ALL involve that!

- Reading the silly, funny, scary, exciting, interesting books – not just the ones I thought were great because they were based on historical characters or events!

I needed to learn that life is bigger than school; bigger than school subjects. Way, *way* bigger! And so much more exciting! Life is richest and most wonderful when there is no expectation or agenda attached to the strewing.

Finally I learned that bringing more of what the children love into their lives is better than trying to balance it out by suggesting something different. By being interested in what interests them, and being interesting myself, our life becomes more ... *interesting*! (It's really not rocket science, is it!)

When I want to suggest something that they are unlikely to stumble upon themselves, it can and should be as natural as the way I might call a friend over to see something cool, or email someone a link to something I think they might like, or buy something for a friend that I know they'd just *love* – even if it's not something I love myself.

From Product Placement to Natural Strewing

We lived in a Christian community once, whose slogan was to let your spiritual life be natural, and your natural life be spiritual. It should be the same with strewing: it moves from "product placement" to "strewing" when our suggestions or scatterings are totally relaxed and natural, when there is no hidden agenda that they should "learn something," no expectation that they should say yes to our suggestion.

So I finally realized that strewing works best when:

- My motivation is simply to share something genuinely cool and awesome that I've discovered!

- I bring things into our world with no strings attached – that's zilch, zero, not even the ones I'm SURE are "invisible"!

- I have no expectation of an enthusiastic YES!

- I embrace any "no, thanks" responses, trusting that it's because, in that moment, they want to do something even more wonderful than what I am offering!

When I bring wonderful, new, different, and intriguing things into our lives without any pressure or expectations, our wonder and enjoyment increases. When I tickle our senses with new smells, tastes, sounds, and objects, we engage more fully with our world. When I spontaneously point something out rather than pre-plan it, they are far more likely to respond with a "Wow, that's cool, Mum!" rather than "What's she up to now?" When I offer a swirling smorgasbord of opportunities and objects because they're wonderful, not because they tick a school box, life is far more delicious!

I eventually realized that I had been looking at my initial question the wrong way entirely. The issue wasn't about finding a balance between activity and passivity on the part of parent and child; it is about being active participants – partners – in this wonderful unschooling life, naturally sharing with each other cool and interesting things we stumble upon along the way!

~ Karen Bieman

15. What Schooly Thing Did You Panic About?

And how were your fears alleviated?

I think my only fear was that my dyslexic oldest would never learn to spell. She could read, it was just hard, but her spelling was *so bad* that the spell checker couldn't understand it. But she picked it up from regularly chatting with friends on Skype while playing Minecraft; they regularly helped her with spelling and after a while she got it.

Now she is a writer, just like her dad and grandfather (her dad is also dyslexic and a writer, who thanks to spellcheck learned to spell at twenty-four or so after being in public school and never learning to spell).

The rest I was sure they would pick up — they had to be better than I was at math no matter what despite me going to public school, and they are. They know way more history than I do regarding multiple subjects, despite me being in public school, thanks to TV triggering their interests (a lot of anime, American cartoons, a lot of sitcoms, just little bits here and there led to surprising amounts of knowledge).

They learned scripture because we talk about it and read together often or have it on audio-book. Literature, languages, some programming, computer comprehension, economics, politics, taking care of the home, cooking, cultures, psychology, so much science – I don't know, they just absorbed all of it. We have so many discussions as my husband as and I are interested or as the kids are interested about whatever and they absorb so much.

~ Heather Young

I had one that I jokingly predicted would never do anything besides video games. The Wii taught him how to do math (scoring different sports) and he learned to read from games as well. Now he's seven and pretty fluent at reading, and for fun he does advanced math puzzles in his spare time when he's not gaming or playing sports.

My other panic was probably that my oldest wouldn't be able to take his mandatory tests when that age arrived. I knew that we didn't teach to the test or use a curriculum so I couldn't picture how his interests could fill in all the gaps. By the time he reached mandatory testing age we had empowered him to own his education though, so he chose to keep unschooling and just took a week at the end of that year to do some practice tests and watch some tutorials and videos about stuff he was unfamiliar with. He did well that first year and hasn't struggled with other years either.

~ Traci Porter

―――――

That they'd be unprepared for college. They were ready and since they are there because they *want* to be, not because it's the next thing to do, *and* because the classroom environment is new, it's actually exciting and interesting to them. The "lack of prep" has turned out to be "lack of burnout!" My daughter is a junior in college and is still excited about her classes! My son is a freshman and loving learning! And two of my other kids chose to go to work after high school: one is a successful graphic designer and the other is a plumber's apprentice. They all find their path!

~ Jessie Lynn

―――――

At first, it was things like *how are they going to learn to meet deadlines or follow instructions?*

Then with our kids who weren't even going to go to school at all, it was *how are they going to learn to read and do math?*

Fears were alleviated through many, many stories shared by families who'd already been through it. Also through the realization that school deadlines and instructions were *not* the only ones in the world and that those things *do* come up in various areas of life and can be just as effectively (if not more so) learned through *those* experiences versus schools' artificially created ones.

~ Stacie Mahoe

―――――

Initially, my biggest fear was reading. I repeatedly read article after article about how kids will teach themselves, how boys typically read later, and other unschooling success stories.

Now, being on *this* side of success, I am grateful for all those who shared their children's stories and offered encouragement to have faith it would happen. My fully autodidactic eleven-year-old is a fluent and joyful reader!

~ T. McCloskey

16. How Do You Share God and Scripture?

My primary way of sharing Christ with my kids is by example – they desire to read their Bibles because they see me and my husband reading ours. They want to go to church – sometimes more than my husband and I want to go! We pray as a family and they have seen firsthand answers to *big* prayers as well as not so big ones.

~ Jessie Lynn

—————

Hmm, I'm not sure if you can "unschool" faith. I see faith as something you either have or you don't. Yes, children can learn the scripture, the meaning of sacraments, but that isn't a guarantee they will have strong faith. And everyone's faith experience is different. My faith will not be my children's. My husband and I show our relationship with God by setting an example, being contributing members of the church body (may or may not include church attendance), and regular family prayer and Bible reading. I already see my fifteen-year-old forming her own opinions and ideas about God. I actually love this. It provides for many interesting debates and discussions. One thing I wish for my children is to question *everything* about what they hear. Turn it over, read, talk, debate, and form their own relationship with God.

~ Karen Bieman

—————

When I think about those scriptures in Deuteronomy I am also reminded about how we are supposed to lead by example. The best way I can teach my kids is to show them by example. It says we are to "pray without ceasing," "love one another," and "answer softly." Am I showing the fruit of the Spirit? Am I being an example in the gifts of the Spirit? Am I speaking the Word over my life and theirs? Am I diligent in my own studies? Am I speaking the Word when I lie down, when I rise up, when I go to the store, when I go to the park?

I find that when I'm doing these things it provides an atmosphere of learning for my children. They are more apt to mimic me, ask dozens of questions, talk about what they think. It provides room for discussions, and from these things they learn! I don't have to create a Bible curriculum for them to learn the Bible. You know what I mean?

~ Amanda Rodgers

A lot of what is described above. Modeling the best we can. Apologizing when we screw up. Reading Scripture on our own. The kids ask to have Bible stories read to them (our daughter is *obsessed* with Jericho!). We just finished over a year supporting a mom who had lost her son to CPS. The kids went with me to court and on many of their supervised visits. It brought a lot of *tough* discussions about grace, forgiveness, love, parenting, etc. I think, really, we don't keep much secret from our kids. We discuss a lot in front of them and they see/hear us pray over situations.

~ Rachel Miller

For us, faith is something my husband and I have, that we can try to explain to our children, but we leave their relationship with God up to them and God (which is basically all you can do anyway). We do go to church, and the kids go to Sunday school. If my kids didn't want to go, we would discuss that with them and I would not want to force my kids into something faith-related that they didn't want to be a part of. As others said, you can't force faith. We try to model our faith inside and outside of church to our kids, because my husband and I both grew up where faith was only something you "did" in church.

If we mess up, we try to apologize. Basically, we are models of our faith, just as we are models of how to behave, think, act, learn, and live.

I am very thankful that so far, our children have, as far as we can tell, developed their own unique faith and relationship with Christ.

I have also been known to "strew" bible learning, etc. My kids pick up a lot, and they really love Sunday school. It's the only "school" we do and I wish regular school was more like Sunday school!

~ Lilly Walsh

———

When I was a kid my punishments often involved writing scripture – I know my mom did the best she knew and hoped the outcome would be that I understood the word of God and applied it to my life. However, it took me until just a few years ago to really begin to enjoy my Bible time, because I viewed reading or studying Bible with punishment – at least subconsciously. My goal with my kiddos is to share the joy and love and grace of Jesus.

So far, they all love the Lord, though my oldest is struggling with life in general (most of that is figuring out how to grow up and be an adult).

~ Jessie Lynn

———

I think unschooling does lend itself to the verses in Deuteronomy: when you walk, lie down, etc. My husband and I show our children what faith looks like for us. We go to church and Sunday school, the kids go AWANA, we read the Bible together, and this is the foundation that is being laid for when that faith question will have to be answered for themselves. I do not use a curriculum or any sort of thing like that at home. My own way of living out my faith is not really methodical. It's more taking each day and knowing Who the giver of life is and Who is the author and finisher of my faith. My parents modeled that and I caught it. My husband and I live our faith out and we model it to our children. I pray they are able to catch it and decide for themselves what their faith will look like. If unschooling is learning by living, then I don't see how this aspect of life and learning cannot be equal to others.

~ Jennifer McGrail

———

Jennifer, I so agree that in order for our kids to "see" our faith and our beliefs, we have to live them when we walk, lie down, etc. All the preaching and teaching can return void, especially if the parents and significant others in a person's life do not live out what they say they believe.

Of my five kids (who were all raised with the same teaching, preaching, and studies) one does not believe at this point in his life. He did in earnest when he was younger, but some events in his preteen and teen years (death of his dad and grandparents, all within a year; a youth leader who was very hurtful; the ambivalence and the hypocrisy in many Christians and church leaders) put him in a place that he lost his faith in Christ and in much of humanity. I believe one day he will return to what he used to know to be true; but until then, we keep living out our faith, allowing him to express his frustrations, anger, concerns, beliefs, loving him unconditionally so that he might one day feel that unconditional love from his heavenly Father and Savior. He has told us how much he respects what we believe and how we live it, and perhaps one day that will override all else.

~ Pam Clark

———

I think we *should* be diligent in teaching this, because it's the one thing the Bible tells us we should make sure our kids know. But does that mean we can't unschool it? No, it doesn't!

Because this sure sounds like unschooling to me:

> *"Talk about [the precepts of God] when you sit at home and when you walk along the road, when you lie down and when you get up. Tie them as symbols on your hands and bind them on your foreheads. Write them on the doorframes of your houses and on your gates."*

It's just about making sure it is a part of your everyday life. Not workbooks and memorization charts and sticker rewards – *life*! Make sure you know it, and make sure you talk about it.

Here's my modernized interpretation of that verse:

"Talk about the precepts of God when you're at home and when you're hanging out at the park, at bedtime and at breakfast. Make sure your phone has the Bible app available, and listen to the Bible on CD in your car."

~ Carma Paden

———

Carma, exactly! It is being diligent. However I think the word diligent may be confused with the schooly academic ideas of a schedule and even curriculum.

~ Jennifer McGrail

———

Yes – diligent could easily be applied to a curriculum, but in the context of the verse I think it's clear that it's not meant that way at all.

~ Carma Paden

———

I agree Carma. I think that many in the homeschool community hear the word diligent and think bookwork and schedules and scopes and sequence yada yada yada. In the scripture we are discussing such ideas were nonexistent.

Children learned with their families, living life together. That sounds a lot like unschooling to me.

~ Jennifer McGrail

――――

Let me start with a story: Driving to pick my husband up at work listening to the radio with my oldest, at age two, sitting in the back seat. I don't even remember what I was listening to though obviously the Christian station. Anyway, I hear the lady on the radio say something about "do you want Jesus in your heart?" then my little two-year-old piped up from the back seat, "I want Jesus in MY heart!"

I was so surprised I nearly pulled over (I was a brand new Christian myself – had only been reading the Bible with understanding for maybe three years but was still very much baby Christian). When we got to my husband's work I talked to my daughter about what she said. She had complete comprehension (well as much as possible; she told me in two-year-old language about how she was a sinner and needed Jesus who died and rose again to fix it and so on – from a two-year-old, and not just mimicking). It was at that point that I realized that God worked out the spiritual life way different than the physical – that having the Holy Spirit meant that you could understand things that didn't seem possible from a maturity perspective. Things continued with her – often God would use my little ones' words to help *me* figure something out spiritually. This same child witnessed at age four to my new two-year-old, and then again at six, when my third child was two. And we saw actual change in behavior in each of them as they grew to love Him.

So yes, we focus on talking about what God is doing in our lives and reading the Bible together. It is a just a family thing where we join together to spend time in prayer and to listen to the Word. We have never used a Bible curriculum and quit going to Sunday school when the kids expressed frustration at the lack of meat in the teaching – one can only listen to the same children's Bible story so many times without finding it boring. We pray together and encourage one another and realize that as Christians we are all on a journey together, that the Holy Spirit gives each of us real understanding and growth that has nothing to do with age.

Basically, Jesus never had a curriculum – He talked, told stories, prayed, encouraged, and very seldom got really angry or raised His voice.

~ Heather Young

––––––––

If I say I'm an unschooler and I'm going to let my kids learn to read at their own pace, and without a curriculum, there are certainly people who think it means I'm going to do nothing to nurture their ability to read and I don't care if they ever learn it or not; but of course as unschoolers we know that the exact opposite is true. Reading is one of the most important things on this earth to me, personally, so I read to my children constantly … starting in the womb! I read to them, my husband read to them, I invited visitors to our home to read to them. I encouraged them to read along with me. We listened to stories in the car. Without ever formally teaching them a single thing about reading, each one of them learned to read over time; some gradually and some quickly, and one I honestly have *no* idea when or how it happened.

So when I say "I unschool the Bible" it certainly doesn't mean that I ignore or neglect or otherwise withhold Bible teaching from my children! Instead it means: instead of using a curriculum, I weave it so inextricably into our daily lives that my kids don't even realize there's another way to live!

~ Carma Paden

17. How Do You Help Guide Your Children to Love the Lord?

So far we have Bible studies, talk about God and his word, and pray together. Then when we go to church it's again school-like. Any advice, words of wisdom you can bestow on me?

Some questions to think about. How are your children responding to the Bible studies you are doing? Are they enjoying them? Do they feel forced to do it? Is it a chore to them, or is it a time the family feels close and connected?

~ Gail Pace

———

We don't. We live our beliefs and principles daily. We talk about and share our whys and why nots naturally as topics, situations, questions and experiences come up. My husband and I each genuinely love the Lord and each came to where we are in relationship with God differently and allow for that in our kids' lives as well.

~ Pam Clark

───────

How you practice your religious beliefs is actually a very personal thing. And for someone to tell you you are wrong even if you see it working is not right. Over the years, one thing I have learned through studying the Bible is that the Bible gives us a path to follow. And when we follow it, it will helps us avoid a lot of the pitfalls in life, a lot of the unnecessary obstacles. It is not so much a book of rules.

Think about it. If you are not making arbitrary rules in your home but you have principles in place, they are there to protect our kids and make life run more smoothly. But I think God also knows that sometimes we are stubborn and want to learn the lessons in life the hard way. He does not turn His back on us during these times. And He also lays out a path of forgiveness and ways to get us back on His chosen path for us. Some people are really stubborn, but He stays there by our side through it all.

Think about the word *relationship*. If you are seeking wisdom from someone you see as very wise – that is, someone you look up to and are respectful of and look at in a way that may even put that person above yourself – you will trust advice from that wise person. And even if you are not sure, you will hold onto that advice in the back of your mind for when you find out your way was wrong and theirs was right.

God is that wise person in our lives, except he is God! And in the Old Testament, all the rules were there to show people that they really can't get through life without God or Jesus because there were just too many rules to follow. They needed his grace and forgiveness and mercy.

~ Gail Pace

18. How Do You Handle People Who Insist on Structured Scripture Study?

I would simply ask them "why?" and see where they take it. Most use verses that are taken out of context or based on faulty doctrine, and rarely do they recognize it because it is what is passed on without real discussion and it fits what has become expected and comfortable.

~ Pam Clark

If it feels forced, then the kids are not going to accept it in their hearts. Seeing it being lived out will have a bigger impact. A belief in God cannot be structured for it to be genuine. I also know that when I have done Bible studies with my son and it went on for a long time as in a couple of months, it felt like drudgery, and I didn't want to do it anymore. I could tell he felt that way too.

~ Gail Pace

We don't do formal studies in our house. We do have a beloved family tradition of reading aloud together, and Bible is one more of those things. We also discuss everything we read, so we've mentored our kids through that, and through knowing it well enough ourselves to bring it into conversation about various life issues, things family or friends are going through, and whatever practical applications arise.

To me that's the essence of Deuteronomy 6: when you rise up, when you lie down, when you walk in the way. It's part of the fabric of life.

As far as learning hermeneutical principles, we talk about approaches to interpretation when we encounter doctrine we disagree with — we explain why, and what we endeavour to do in order to form our opinions, rather than just enforcing our opinions. It's really important that the kids hear about how to put principles into action so that they can do it for themselves and not be crippled with dependence on other people's statements, however authoritative they may sound.

~ Erica C. Maine

We don't do set Bible study. We have never set out to teach the Bible. We have always had many different resources around that were available if someone wanted to do particular studies (strewing). We have read from the Bible, from different versions and from children's Bible storybooks as often as they have been desired.

We have conversations, studies based on pertinence to everyday events as the kids have wanted. They have read on their own, been part of youth groups in the past, but to create a special time to "learn" the Bible, to create a curriculum of sorts of it, we just don't. With three young adult children, and two teens, they decide how they want to pursue their relationship with the Lord. We walk ours every day, and they know we are here for and with them as they have questions, concerns, and we have some great discussions off and on, along the way. We have discussed, and they have researched different worldviews and have a great understanding of what and why they believe what they do.

Our youngest is four. We don't do Bible study with him. He doesn't yet have the concept of God, but we do talk about how we were created, the world was created, and answer questions of his wonderment at his age appropriate understanding. We will always have the resources and opportunity available for him, and will naturally discuss and study things as it intertwines in and through all areas of life.

~ Pam Clark

As someone who was made to do devotionals as a kid, I've only *now* begun to find my own way of getting my personal time with God in. But it comes in *so* many forms and ways and times. If I need more dedicated time, I take it. But, like eating, I never dictate that time by a clock. Every day I need to eat. Every day, I have time with God. For me, it's finally become something that's woven into life. In all my years growing up in private schools and church, I've never felt so close to Him nor so strong in my faith.

~ Stacie Mahoe

———

I say that first off, this is a proverb, not a command nor a promise. It's of the same type as "early to bed, early to rise makes a man healthy, wealthy, and wise." Proverbs are little nuggets of general wisdom. They are not laws from God.

Secondly, the more literal translation of that verse would read "educate a child according to his nature and he will not depart from it." That puts a very different spin on it, doesn't it?

~ Mariellen Menix

———

This is from a Jewish Rabbi about Proverbs 22:6 (train up a child in the way he should go or the way he is bent):

"The essence of education, however, is planting, enabling a child to develop in his own way, to utilize his own strengths and character traits, to grow on his own. This is chanoch lana'ar al pi darko, educate a child according to his own way. As the Vilna Ga'on comments, forcing a child against his nature, even if successful at first, is a recipe for unmitigated disaster. Like planting, chinuch requires patience. When bringing up my own wonderful,

172

sometimes-rambunctious children, of whom my wife and I are exceedingly, and I hope rightfully, proud, I would repeat over and over again – patience."

~ Aadel Bussinger

———

Get to the root of your "why" behind believing that you *need* to do so. What is your purpose for doing so? Is this in alignment with how the kids learn, how they want to learn, what other options and choices can be considered.

~ Pam Clark

———

I wouldn't worry about that. I'm far more concerned that they have exposure to the Scriptures and hear how it all fits with real life than that they "study" anything. Our youngest has taken to listening to radio preaching by choice, and one of our daughters chooses to attend the Bible study with us. They each did so in response to their own needs. That they know how to access many forms of support is important to me.

~ Erica C. Maine

19. How Did Your Unschooled Kids Learn to Read?

This is my youngest child's story. She finally nailed the reading thing at a later age than her older brother, so there were more challenges in terms of learning to trust that she was learning in just the right way, at just the right time, for her.

Their two stories are a great contrast to my second oldest, who attended school until he was eight years old. When he came home, he could already read. He has been taught using a very boring phonics program. He hated reading. I used to ask him to read aloud to me, before we discovered unschooling.

One day, he was dutifully reading a chapter book to me while I washed dishes (I was very proud of my multitasking!). After a little while, I realized that the story wasn't making much sense and I commented on it. He sheepishly admitted that he was skipping pages to "get it over with more quickly."

That was the last book I asked him to read aloud, and the last time I expected him to read.

He only read a handful of books after that, but when he did read, he read them because he wanted to. Eventually he decided that reading was hard work for him, and that he had trouble concentrating on the story because of focusing on the skill of reading. He didn't read books again for quite a while, although he did peruse magazines occasionally, about body-boarding or skating.

I recently went into his room and noticed a very interesting book on his bed head and made a joke, saying, "You're not reading a book, are you?" (My teens love humour.) It turns out one of his friends had been reading it, and he'd borrowed it, gotten totally hooked within the first few pages, and decided to buy his own copy.

It's been lovely to see him gradually, gradually recover from the way he experienced reading in the school environment and then, later, in a homeschool environment. It has been amazing to see the difference between his experience of reading, and that of his younger brother and sister, who have always unschooled.

~ Karen Bieman

I have four kids. I read to them; they began to read. Actually, the two youngest picked it up when their older brother, my dyslexic who didn't start reading until age nine, began reading them comic books at bedtime.

~ Carma Paden

———

My middle daughter loved looking at books and would pretend to read them. She showed an interest in letters and their sounds at around age six so I showed her Starfall.com. She quickly caught onto that and was reading simple words. I would help her write out her name and other small words when she would ask.

She listened to a lot of audiobooks, lots of reading being done in the house by older sister and by mom and dad. Visits to the library for fun all the time. I read out loud to the girls and we attended family book discussions. So a *lot* of reading and literature happening in the house naturally without any pressure on her to hurry up and read.

Then she just started taking off, shortly before she turned seven. I realized she was fluent when she read "no loitering" in the bathroom and didn't need help with pronunciation. She read signs everywhere we went. And started reading and chatting on the computer with friends through Skype, Minecraft, Roblox.

She continues to ask when she needs help spelling a word; her writing is improving from when she plays store with her little brother. She likes to write notes and stories. Just the other day I noticed she is starting to type whole sentences, spelled mostly correct, in the chat in Minecraft. I mention the writing because I think a lot of kids actually write before they read. It's all intertwined in the real world and it just seemed that her writing and reading developments came together in spurts.

~ Aadel Bussinger

———

I just asked my seventeen-year-old how he learned to read. "I don't remember. You taught me my letters, I learned how they sound and what words they formed, and the rest is history. Some took longer, and some just came."

Alphabet colouring books, YouTube clips of Sesame Street's two-headed monsters doing basic spelling and phonetics, and most of all, lots and lots and lots of reading aloud to them.

We read a picture Bible to them every night. It was one of the few things my husband would absolutely always do with them, no matter how busy and overwhelmed he was. For my part, storybooks and chapter books, library books, computer screen reading aloud on anything of interest that comes up ... the main thing is that they associate it with togetherness and enjoyment.

They're now ages seventeen down to twelve, and will still gather around for a good children's book if the author is skilled and entertaining. (Kate DiCamillo is a favorite. And lately, we killed ourselves laughing at Neil Gaiman's *Fortunately, the Milk*.)

~ Erica C. Maine

———

My oldest was severely dyslexic, and eclectically homeschooled until about nine. Me being a special ed teacher, I put a lot of pressure early on and it took me a while to deschool.

She really learned basically from playing lots of Nintendo games (and constantly needing help until she didn't anymore) and falling in love with Calvin and Hobbes and then with Minecraft; she and her friends regularly chatter in game. Once she was motivated by her friends it didn't take long after that for her spelling and reading to drastically improve.

My middle child learned to read entirely alone at about six years old. My oldest was very sick in the hospital and while I was busy dealing with that, my middle child just started reading. It just all fell into place without any actual teaching at all. It was amazing to me because I firmly believed children needed to be taught to read and here was my middle child suddenly reading every single chapter book in the house. I started having to put books up that were too intense or not age appropriate.

My youngest just started reading at about ten. He knew the basics (he liked workbooks and Hooked on Phonics – he had his own way of using them but loved doing them). He listened to audiobooks all the time. I didn't teach him to read at all. He just picked it up a little here a little there. We had lots of closed captioning on tv (I need it on so it is always on), lots of audio books, lots of computer games – we read aloud the bits needed until he was able to do it himself. And then suddenly he wasn't just reading but was reading big words without even noticing.

Now at twelve he has suddenly had it all click as far as spelling too. He no longer refuses to type but instead just asks how and I give him the word rules with it if any apply. "Wow, I didn't know that!" Then he adds that word to his "list of words he now can spell." This is my super cautious kid who wants to make sure everything is right before he does it, so it isn't surprising he was the slowest to really get started.

It was just really a case for all three of waiting till their brains were ready and then it all fell into place.

~ Heather Young

———

Books were and are our thing. We filled our home with books, labeled common household items, turned on and left on the closed captioning. We read stories together from the time the kiddos were born, all the time – during the day, at bedtime, waiting in lines. I'm sure it helped in some way that they saw me toting a book of my own *all the time*.

We noticed our son could read when he was about four. I remember the moment his speech therapist asked us if we knew he could read – she and we were incredulous. I knew he loved books but due to his communication struggles (he's hearing impaired and took awhile to sign and talk) I hadn't noticed he could actually read.

Our daughter was about five when she asked me to read a book to her. Mid-story I paused for some reason and she continued reading the story. She looked at me with wide eyes and said "I can read!" She went to get another book and another one, checking to see if she could read those!

~ Dana Tanaro Britt

———

I think in a sense, everyone learns to read the same way: by watching their parents, by being read to, by appreciating stories, by being surrounded by the written word, by playing with colors and letters and numbers and shapes, by finding patterns in the world around them. I think the biggest difference between my three boys is just the catalyst that really put them past the tipping point from *learning* to read to actually *being* a reader.

For my oldest, it was Dr. Seuss books. He loved Dr. Seuss, and we read them to him every night, over and over. Eventually he was reading them on his own. My middle son has always loved computers, and has used one competently from the time he was a toddler. So it's no surprise that he learned to read largely through computer games. My third son was a few years older than the others before he really started reading. The thing that really made it "click" for him, besides just being ready, was Facebook and Skype and wanting to talk to his friends. He reads quite well now, and spells beautifully, and is getting better all the time, through self-motivated good old-fashioned practice.

~ Jennifer McGrail

———

I didn't use any reading materials or require reading, and my boy read in spite of it. But my girl is just now learning at six, so I have no post for her. She wanted to do the Book-It program with her brother, and she's pretty competitive so she didn't want me to read it to her if he was reading himself. She's struggling some but she doesn't get too frustrated because she stops when she's annoyed and she isn't required to do anything so she comes back when she's calm. We've always had reading time as a family where I'll read aloud while they do whatever, or I'll read bedtime stories. Reading has always been treated as a fun and voluntary activity here so as yet, nobody hates it as long as they are reading about stuff that they love.

~ Traci Porter

20. How Do Unschooled Kids Learn Harder Math?

I haul my calculator with me every time I go grocery shopping. I was drilled and tested and I still can't do the times tables. I think there is a huge difference between "knowing how to multiply" and "having factors memorized." I know how to multiply, and much more. Understanding mathematical functions is not the same as committing a large set of problems to memory for ease and simplicity. Some people can memorize numbers like that. Some can't. I know a few simple multiplication problems. So I take my phone with me everywhere, which has a handy calculator. I've never felt that I was missing anything in life. In fact, I do large problems and calculations all the time.

Part of the problem with "they will never choose to learn time tables on their own" is the assumption that they are necessary for life, and that they won't be able to function without them. The other problem is not trusting the child. They don't see the times tables as important even if they use math everyday in their projects? I think you could offer it as a tool for them, and strew resources for them to pick up that skill, but forcing is not the answer.

~ Aadel Bussinger

———

I didn't learn times tables (learned a system to figure them out that I came up with myself) until I was homeschooling. We bought Times Tales (the kids really wanted it) and we all loved it. We can all do upper times tables because of it (I nearly failed math in sixth grade because I couldn't memorize long enough to pass on the test – once I finally did I promptly forgot it).

So if you really are concerned about multiplication even though so many of us didn't learn them (neither did my dad and he was a math major in college and *taught* math – he eventually learned them thanks to constant use) then I would back off for a while then strew Times Tales and do it as a fun game together (if you bring it in immediately they will hate it). Also fun is Number Rings (a game where you add, subtract, divide, multiply to get to each number on your board – kind of like math bingo), and mine all play Dungeons and Dragons and Minecraft and use multiplication and division all the time in those.

~ Heather Young

———

I still can't do my times tables in my head (except for a select few). Only time I ever needed them that badly was in school. I'm not crippled in life, that's for sure. Every phone has a calculator now.

On the other hand, I can multiply any number combination of any size on paper as well with a cool method that my math teacher taught me. I just don't memorize things when it comes to math. Never have been able to.

(And multiplication rock is awesome if you are looking to strew.)

~ Lilly Walsh

Unschooling means they are learning what they need as they need it, therefore they are picking things up at a different speed from the "set in stone" schedules everyone makes for kids. Grade levels are there as a construct for organizing information and children – behavior management for the classroom in order to simplify things. When we had one-room schoolhouses, kids moved up in level as they were ready, not according to age. When you realize that "grade level" is only something used regularly in the last century and that up till then everything was based on "child level" it makes it easier to not compare.

~ Heather Young

I think it's more important to show our kids that they *can* learn anything at anytime, not that they must know something at a certain time. I know that I still teach myself math concepts to make life easier. Most of the math I learned in school (equations) is pretty useless to me right now in my life. Simple concepts that

I've used over and over in life have been reinforced through my own need for them.

If these math concepts are a basic need for life, then I think we can trust that our kids will learn them. They may ask for help when they use them at first, and we can help them learn them. Most unschoolers are not just going to give up on basic life skills just because they weren't taught them at a certain age, not if we have fostered the mindset that anyone can learn something at any time.

That's also why I think it's more important to give our kids real-life opportunities rather than worry about giving them something to learn at home. Doing things in life (alongside us or other adults, etc.) will require them to learn the skills they need.

~ Lilly Walsh

————

I think it's far, far more important for kids to love learning, and to know that they can learn anything they want to know anytime they want to know it than it is to learn some set of facts. There are tons of multiplication facts I don't remember off the top of my head, and never once have I felt crippled by it. I understand the math *concepts* (which I never understood or appreciated until I was an adult, by the way, and got rid of all the math phobia that school had bestowed on me) and I know how to quickly find answers when I need them.

My fifteen-year-old is like me – more of an idea person than a number person – and doesn't have any times tables memorized. But I don't worry at all, because like me, he knows the concepts, he knows how to work things out in his head, he knows how to find answers, and he knows how to use a calculator. My twelve-year-old is like his dad, and finds numbers really really fun, so I don't worry about him either. And the eight- and four year-olds are learning all the math they need in their daily lives, just like their brothers did before them.

If someone *wants* to sit down and memorize times tables, and/or finds it useful for their own purposes, their own style of learning, etc, great. But there is definitely no blanket reason for *everyone* to do so, especially if it requires rote drill, force, etc, like it always did for me. All it did for me was make me (1) hate math, and (2) think I was no good at math. It took *years* to undo both.

~ Jennifer McGrail

———

I'm one who does all multiplication in my head as well. I use part memorization and part just multiplying in my head. My husband knows his tables but he needs a calculator to figure out a tip at a restaurant. Or he'll ask me. I do see how it's an advantage. Necessary? As others have said, probably not. But definitely an advantage to know how to multiply.

I would suggest putting them in some real life situations that call for multiplication. Take them to a yard sale and let them buy a few items of the same price to practice on. Have them build or measure some stuff in the metric system so that they figure out the system of tens. Can they count by twos, fives, etc? If not then have them help you roll change and if they can figure out how to do it they can share in the value with you (showing them how to count two pennies at a time, a nickel at a time, etc.)

~ Traci Porter

Just to put some perspective on the whole memorization thing – when I was a kid in public school, my family moved across the state midway into the year that we were supposed to memorize the multiplication tables. I went from a school where I knew everything up to my 6s to a school where they were done memorizing multiplication facts. So I didn't memorize the 7s through 12s. But I understood how multiplication worked and was still able to do the math. Over time I eventually did memorize some of those oft-used multiplication facts I didn't already know just from frequent use, but some of them I still can't rattle off. If you said to me, "Quick, what's 8 times 7?" it would take me a minute without a calculator to come up with 56. I don't have it memorized but I can arrive at it fairly quickly because I know 8 times 6 is 48 then I add 10 and subtract 2 and arrive at 56. Is it as "efficient" as memorizing all the facts? No. But it works and as rarely as I use that particular fact it works pretty well.

~ Mariellen Menix

My point is that comprehension and general numeracy are more important to me than memorizing facts. The memorization occurred for me through the process of life.

We haven't ever public schooled but my seven-year-old has a lot of public school friends. He hates it when they know how to do things that he doesn't. They'll be discussing stuff that they did in school and they'll say "have you done xyz yet?" And he hates having to say no. He's requested curriculum before but I haven't gone that route because when I borrowed one to test drive he just kind of played with it but didn't want to do it anyway. (He's asleep now at 10:30am; not really the driven type!) If I were in your shoes, I would just give them what they want. I'd find curricula or whatever, tell them this is what the public school grade level is but that you aren't using that as a gauge. Tell them that if they want to learn some of that stuff you'll help them. Still no tests or schedule or anything but if they want to learn what public school kids are learning I think I'd let them. These days I think anything that encourages a kid not to self-doubt is good though, so try to explain that everyone learns differently at different times and that's a good thing.

~ Traci Porter

———

I also wanted to add that when a child is intrinsically motivated to learn something, they generally do so quickly and easily. My eight-year-old had never done any sort of math problem on paper in his life, and one day he asked me to help him find a website where he could practice math. I signed him up at Khan Academy, and he started at the most basic, and worked his way up. He loved it. In one day, he'd literally taught himself many school years worth of math.

~ Jennifer McGrail

20a. A Note About Math

One of the questions we run into a lot, as a radically unschooling family, is how kids will learn higher level math if they aren't forced to learn the math facts traditionally, especially if they want to go to college and go into a math or science field.

Though my husband chose not to go to college he is in a math field: 3-D object-oriented programming requires a ton of math, everything from trigonometry, geometry, and algebra to physics. He uses maths regularly, usually in his head without ever looking up formula.

This is a man who never took more than business math in school (and never did homework there – you can read about his experience in his autobiography, which is listed in the resources at the end of the book). It took him just a few weeks to teach himself algebra and trigonometry so he could understand a concept in C++. He is completely self-taught in programming and maths, and he does it because he loves it.

Not only that, but he understands what he knows well enough to talk about it in a way that non-programmers can understand – and apparently enjoy – what he is talking about, if his blog is any indication.

The thing about math that most people don't even realize is that once you get past "learning math" – especially in math and science fields – it is mostly creative, conceptual problem solving rather than just "knowing the facts."

You do learn the facts, but that is because you use them regularly. If you can't remember something, you look it up. My husband has memorized a lot of formulas, now but that is because he uses them daily, not because he memorized them for a test. Our kids play with numbers with him regularly because it is fun and it is a natural part of life. Also, there is a ton of math use when drawing and painting – I use math regularly when I paint.

There is a huge difference between boring, black-and-white facts and conceptual math. The difference between memorizing math facts and using conceptual math is like the difference between knowing how to diagram a sentence and knowing how to form a beautiful one. Diagramming a sentence may be useful but it won't help you communicate with written language.

Then there are word meanings, the etymology of words, homonyms and homophones and synonyms, and all sorts of things that go well beyond basic sentence structure and colloquialisms, and, and, and ...

These are the things that make words and language fun. Math is the same way.

At the moment of this writing my ten-year-old son is considering how he could build Frank Lloyd Wright's "Falling Water" in Minecraft, drawing the ideas on graph paper (complete with ruler), and deciding whether it can be done at all.

What we laypeople think of as *math* is not what people in mathematics fields think of as *math*. I say this as a non-math person myself: I am a word person surrounded by people who love numbers and play with them all the time and who work in the field.

My brothers play with math regularly. My middle brother worked at NASA as an electrical engineer until just last month thanks to the changes in the program; my other brother is going into metal fabrication and blacksmithing and you would not believe the number use in that.

My dad was a math major in college (traditionally schooled) and a math teacher until he took on computers. My dad almost failed math all through school because he had no memory for "facts" but when he got to college and past the "basic math" he fell in love with the logic and concepts and the fact that math is really just playing with numbers and figuring things out.

My dad says, "You can always look up the facts if you need them; the important part is being able to play with numbers."

Once you start noticing it you see math everywhere, from perspective (how it seems the building is bigger the closer you are) and the math involved in building that structure to the math used to calculate speed in the cars or how much the gas costs per gallon to the arch of the rainbow. It is how our world is designed.

Part of deschooling is learning to see math not as scary numbers but rather as a different way of thinking and seeing the world. Math is everywhere and part of everything and learning to see it as patterns and rhythms and part of how God created the world, part of the very structure, allows us to no longer fear it or teach our children to fear it.

~ Heather Young

21. What Can They Learn from
_____?

Pick your favorite non-educational thing and talk about what YOUR kids learned from it.

We watched Monuments Men the other night. Didn't have to explain the beach at Normandy to the kids at all. They knew it from a video game re-enacting D-Day. It made me think of the similar learning done in medieval reenactments. Plus they got a quick education in European art, geography, and edifices from the movie itself.

I've also noticed they know a lot of ancient culture basics from playing Civilization, like which rulers are from which cultures or regions.

~ Erica C. Maine

Hetalia. Hetalia. Hetalia. Their obsessive watching lead to fan fiction writing has lead not only to actual writing, including basic grammar, plot development, character development, character design, story arcs, and so on. Basically we have had conversations that you generally don't run into till senior-year college writing courses. Add in excessive knowledge of countries, WWI, and WWII – to the point where they have corrected my history buff mother-in-law on numerous occasions. Discussions of cultures and how they affect country personality, politics, etc. Hetalia also led to developing their manga drawing skills – and both are moving towards careers in writing and drawing because of it.

Not to mention developing their cosplay skills and making them want to cosplay more. Hetalia may even be considered the impetus to friendships, willingness to go to crowded anime conventions, willingness to start online business, and so on.

~ Heather Young

This was kinda tough as I have a harder time not seeing the value in virtually everything. I can talk myself in circles on what a person can learn from any and everything.

Okay so, I think I have something that's not "educational" in and of itself (even though I can argue otherwise): Korean pop music and their videos. Of course, she has picked up lots of Korean, can identify which characters are Korean or Chinese or Japanese.

She knows lots about the culture and it has led her to a universal language that has no ties to any native land: Esperanto. She's learning that language and is even teaching another home-schooled friend. They are speaking back and forth. She's also found people online to speak with.

~ Patrice London

———

The kids have been watching a Lego series on Netflix. They now know that "Chi" refers to one's energy and that it is a Chinese concept. Because he asked me a question about it, we had a little discussion and he knows that I learned more about chi when my husband and oldest daughter took kung fu for a bit years ago.

My four-year-old knows about great white sharks and hammer-head sharks because of the *Hungry Shark Evolution* game which his brother and dad play (and the movie *Sharknado*).

My nine-year-old son just learned that you can look up gaming questions on the internet and is keeping me updated on how much money he's earned in *Hungry Shark Evolution* and how much more he needs in order to buy the next bigger shark. It's also fun to hear him and his dad discuss ways to handle different situations that come up in the game. He has always been inter-ested in sharks so, due to various shark movies and games (not documentary types), he knows all kinds of facts about sharks.

~ Stacie Mahoe

———

Nintendo 64 *Paper Mario* and *Mario 64* – a lot of reading. And of course puzzle solving. And determination to get to the next level and also a desire to master by revisiting the game several times over the years.

Unrestricted time online has taught my kids how to research, they often compare and contrast items they wish to buy, sometimes putting months of research in, to ensure the best deal and best product for their money.

~ Jessie Lynn

———

Patrice, Esperanto has great personal significance for my family! My grandparents met and fell in love at the Esperanto club in England after WWII.

My grandfather's journal was written in Esperanto – he missed a ton of school due to polio as a child, and writing in English never became easy for him. The relative simplicity of the language's rules enabled his literacy.

My grandmother translated it to English years later. We also have her handwritten journal that she kept to keep herself from going crazy while they were emigrating to Canada – he went first and she missed him horribly. It was mostly in English with mundane daily notes, but her most personal and sad romantic thoughts were written in Esperanto.. I suppose she thought it would be private, but she brought us to Canada. We learned enough French that we can catch the gist even without an Esperanto dictionary. Very sweet and sad all at once.

~ Erica C. Maine

Jessie, I see those same benefits here too. My children research everything. By the time they come to me about something, they have it all together. When my oldest was interested in switching dance schools, she'd already narrowed it down to two choices before I knew she was interested in moving on. When she read Robin Hood, she fell in love with archery, found that our local 4-H organization offered it free of charge, then she came to me saying she was interested in doing it. I thought I would have to search for a class but she had it all together. All I had to do was take her. She had even written to the group and when she came to me, had the mail from them about their upcoming open house to sign up for clubs.

~ Patrice London

I guess I will just say that there has never been one single game played, one single movie or TV show watched, one single Youtube video viewed that they did not learn something. They have continually brought all kinds of subject matter to my attention over the years and I'll ask, "Where did you learn that?" and some game, book, magazine, movie... is mentioned. I have no concern at all that people learn. Period. When we start determining important things to learn, someone is going to miss out on something. Encourage it all, and more and more is built upon by bits and pieces and soon large, whole ideas are there. They often have information on things I have never, ever learned.

~ Pam Clark

What can they learn from *Portal* or *Portal 2*? Physics (Newtonian and non-Newtonian), problem solving, spatial skills, critical thinking, fine and gross motor development, plot development and character writing, math, chemistry, biology, and how to make awesome gloves (which involves its own set of new skills and knowledge).

What can they learn from *Bridezillas*? Conflict resolution, emotional management, moderation vs. excess, frugality vs. spend thriftiness, fashion design, party planning and event management and coordination, what sort of qualities to look for in a friend/mate, and more.

~ Mariellen Harris Menix

————

SpongeBob led to an interest in Texas, geography, the science of "breathing" underwater, and if jellyfish really made jelly.

~ Aadel Bussinger

————

Yes, the Percy Jackson series is what led my then ten-year-old to read the comic book version of *The Odyssey*, among other things.

Really, fantasy fiction novels in general. My middle child is like me and loves to read. And is a fount of random information, and ideas, mostly gleaned from every book in the house, library, and pretty much everywhere else. My own understanding of math, history, science, mythology, fairy tales, and so on, is a result of all the fiction reading I do, my kid is the same way. (The current young adult fantasy I am reading is all about geometry, in a magical way which makes it palatable for me because not keen on it as a science.) I can't stand reading real-life stories because too often they hurt my heart and make me depressed. Throw a tiny bit of magic or fantasy in there and suddenly I can cope with it because it isn't real and glean so much about the real world from the stories.

~ Heather Young

Mariellen, I don't know if they learn conflict resolution from *Bridezillas* – at least none I've seen! Unless you watch the show and do the opposite. That show makes me wonder how they got engaged at all!

~ Gail Pace

You put your finger on it, Gail. They watch and talk about what went wrong and what could have been done better. And yes, the girls often wonder how the people on the show got engaged. It's also spurred many conversations about what each thinks it's important to look for in a mate.

~ Mariellen Harris Menix

I'll use an example from a few years back when we first started officially unschooling and let go of screen limits. My oldest son was about five at the time and he absolutely loved *Free Willy* and would watch all of the *Free Willy* movies over and over. This led to a very deep interest in whales, which then led to a deep interest in all sea life. We proceeded to watch many documentaries on whales and sea life, buy books, and do research. He can tell you more facts about whales than anyone I know. Over the last few years this has developed into a love of animal facts for him and my second son, and also got him interested in survival skills. He also loves learning about weather and anything in nature, but the real kick starter to all of this came through us letting him watch *Free Willy* to his little heart's content.

~ Lilly Walsh

———

My oldest was a late reader due to severe dyslexia plus some neurological stuff that made her have general high stress all the time. She loved playing Wii games but couldn't read so we would read them for her, or my middle child would, who loved watching and loved reading. They would make up stories while they played together or my middle child would just read what the oldest needed as she played. After a while she stopped needing so much help until finally she stopped asking for help at all. Basically those games taught her to read.

They also lead to many things. Knowledge of all sorts of fish and bugs – instant recognition, even in the real world (*Animal Crossing* and *Harvest Moon*). Interest in dinosaurs and dinosaur bones (*Animal Crossing*). Understanding of economy, saving, stock market, spending, loans, working to pay off loans, value of different items being dependent on need and quality (*Animal Crossing* and *Harvest Moon*), interest in constellations and how they got named (*Animal Crossing*), interest in taking care of animals, what is accurate in game and what isn't (*Harvest Moon*), ability to do things on a schedule (*Harvest Moon*), tracking needs, goals, planning ahead (*Harvest Moon* and *Animal Crossing* to a lesser degree), spreadsheets, research, reading guides on paper and online (*Harvest Moon* and to lesser degree *Animal Crossing*).

~ Heather Young

22.

What's Something You Loved that Led to Learning?

When I was a teen I was a passionate escapist reader. I went through a stage where I read every YA book our library had, one per night, because I wanted to completely escape my life, especially school. One book I read was about a young piano player who lost her hearing or went blind. She passionately loved the new song, "Rhapsody in Blue," and desperately wanted to learn to play it but was dealing with the loss and was sure she would never play again. That character's passion for "Rhapsody in Blue" led to my finding it and listening to it, which lead to a life-long love of classical music and exploration of many music types and styles that I had not been exposed to while growing up.

~ Heather Young

I got into internet marketing (which led to blogging and social media marketing and email marketing etc) because I was spending a lot of time on forums talking story with other moms and having your own website was a hot topic at that time.

So I wanted to try it. Made my first website back in 2002 I think, with a free host by learning HTML code via a website I found and hand coding everything. So all of that was completely free. From there it just progressed to where I am now:

- built a small network of sites and sold it

- have three main websites now, all built with WordPress

- creating selling e-books online (including one for kindle)

- running a membership site

- social media and email work for others

- running and growing my own sites

~ Stacie Mahoe

Reading and watching science fiction (pure science fiction, not fantasy) really got me into philosophy and thinking about ethics, worldview, etc. It also really helped me analyze literature because I could think about the "what-ifs" and dissect the plot.

~ Aadel Bussinger

Stacie, that is funny. I got into web design and hosting because I was writing and my husband made me a website. He set up a site for me for my birthday, probably in 2001? But then never had time to do anything on it, so I got sick of waiting and learned to do it myself. So trial and error lead to me learning CSS, HTML, PHP, graphic design, which led to me doing book covers, selling my artwork online, selling prints of my work on t-shirts and bags, web design, doing all the publishing stuff for my husband's books, writing and publishing my own book, and now to me fussing around with a program for making visual novels.

Aadel, same here, all my science fiction and fantasy reading has lead me to better understand history, economics, politics, as well as philosophy.

~ Heather Young

And of course, now I'm pursuing a degree in psychology. That was an outpouring of many years of research in alternative education, history, philosophy, and teaching and leading people at church.

~ Aadel Bussinger

I developed a passion for history from tacky pulp novels. Even Anne Rice type stuff. I learned everything I could find about ancient Persia because I read *Servant of the Bones*. Ireland was because of a spate of trashy romance novels that I can't even remember now. The lowest of the pulp press drew me to classics.

~ Mariellen Menix

Watching anime (my pretend friend was Speed Racer when I was four) later led to a passion for both Japanese and Korean culture. I now love watching Korean dramas and learning the Korean language, culture, and history thanks to k-dramas.

When I was a teen, reading Mary Stewart's *Merlin* series lead to my passion for King Arthur stories, which is what lead me into British history, British TV, reading Old English, and writing (it lead to my first major writing success as a teen because I wrote about something I was passionate about which got me my first A).

~ Heather Young

Taking karate led to studying Japanese language, culture, calligraphy, and alphabets for a while. We had an actual Japanese sensei or two higher up in the organization and used some Japanese words in the classroom. Our local senseis taught us a bit about Japanese politeness so we would understand why the head senseis acted the way they did. I've just always loved it.

Now, I'd like to borrow Oriental touches for redecorating my small new house (if and when I get around to it) because it can be so clean and peaceful.

~ Erica C. Maine

———

Reading – just reading, in general, mostly fiction, and science fiction (okay, and yes, romance too), every spare minute since I was five – has taught me a huge amount of history and philosophy, put me well over the ninetieth percentile in size of vocabulary, and taught me how the English language works. Grammar was always a snap, so I took Advanced English Grammar in college as a fun – yes, fun! – elective, and took Latin as my language (our grammar rules and huge swaths of our vocabulary are based on Latin).

Later, with no actual training other than my own exploration into the topic, I was able to land a job as a freelance proofreader for an educational publishing company, and I took that experience and got a full-time job as publications editor at another publishing house.

~ Carma Paden

———

I love to read, and have read a lot of books others may find questionable, whether in religious content, or romance/sex, from a young age. I was introduced to porn the summer before sixth grade. I did not know what I was to be reading when the new neighbor kids offered them to me to read. They were from their dad's stash of books and magazines. They were there for whomever, so the kids shared the books with me, knowing I liked to read. So, off and on over a year or so, I read them. They did not lead me to addiction, nor to a desire to continue to read them. They did answer some questions I had, exposed me to some things I knew I would never do or want to watch others do. They did not entice me to look at magazines, watch pornographic movies. They just were.

They did lead me to be open to finding answers in unexpected places, whether in a new genre of reading, or in movies, games, from other people, within churches and synagogues, clubs, or wherever. Not about pornography, but about everything. When you take stigma away, one is much more open to opening (or closing) options before them, based on their own personal beliefs or interests or ignorance with a desire to be less so, and not out of shame or fear or tradition or expectation or someone else's beliefs; finding one's own way for one's own calling.

I did not have a lot of parental oversight during those years. There were six kids, both parents working, and the times were just different. My parents were very traditional in their parenting and punishment, so I did not share a lot of things I did or wondered about, if I knew it would cause distress or bring on harsh discipline. That also has brought me to a different way of doing things now. I studied the end result and ripple effects of our own traditional parenting with our oldest kids, and found it troublesome at best, and relationship-damaging at worst.

From that we learned and changed, and now my kids may not share everything with us, but they do know that they can come to us without fear of shame or punishment if they do something that they know we would not comfortably support. They know we have learned, have had a huge paradigm shift and value them, their questions, their thoughts, their dreams, and we are there for them in the good, the bad, and the ugly. Together we can sift through it all, and find a way to make the necessary or desired changes in their lives.

~ Pam Clark

23. Unschooling a Special Needs Child

A moment of doubt.

The room was nearly silent. The awkwardness was palpable. Even the speech therapist ... bubbly, outgoing and friendly until just a few weeks prior, absolutely refused to look us in the eye, instead staring down at some imaginary spot on the table. I remember looking at the clock – a standard issue, one-in-every-room school clock – and watching the second hand slowly sweep around until I heard the audible click that signified that another excruciatingly long minute had gone by.

There were five of us gathered around the table: my husband and me, a speech therapist, an occupational therapist, and some sort of head of the special education department. We were there to discuss the next course of action for our then four-year-old first child. He'd started to resist their recommended therapies, crying at every session. They were strongly recommending a special needs preschool, and were in visible disagreement when we declined. They thought he was too attached to me, and that I needed to "be strong" and let him go.

It wasn't destined to be a happy meeting of the minds.

He needed the socialization! He needed to catch up! He needed more intensive therapy! He needed to learn to separate from mom and dad!

I felt sick. I'd never questioned our decision to unschool until that very moment. But in that room, under that fire, I questioned. Not only was our schooling decision under harsh critique, so too was my job as a mother. He was having issues separating because of me. They weren't able to do their job because of me. He wasn't going to reach his full potential because of me. I couldn't breathe. Couldn't even speak for fear of crying (that would come later in the car). My heart told me one thing, and my head told me not to listen. Was unschooling really the right decision? Should we send him to the special ed preschool after all? It felt as though his entire life hinged on that very moment.

One week later, our choice was clear. We'd reached an impasse with his therapists, and the current situation was no longer going to work. Everybody involved was miserable, most notably our son. We pulled him out of the system, renewed our decision to unschool, and didn't look back.

That meeting was eleven years ago. I have never, even for a moment, even in the darkest corners of my mind, regretted our decision. Unschooling was the best choice we ever made, not just for that son, but for all of our children. And when people ask if unschooling is really suited for a child deemed "special needs," I do not hesitate.

Unschooling would work for any child, but it works especially well for a child with special needs. (And it should be noted too, that when it comes to unschooling there really is no such thing as "special needs." We all have our own unique needs.) By its very nature, it is a completely individualized, personalized, respectful path; one that takes into account differences in personality, temperament, and learning styles. It is a way to fully honor and support your child – any child – and unschooling has allowed me to watch my son, along with his three siblings, soar and grow into who he is. Not who I want him to be, or who the schools want him to be, or who the "experts" want him to be … but who He wants him to be.

When I think of that meeting, of that day eleven years ago, I only wish I hadn't doubted … even if the doubt began and ended in the very same room. I wish I hadn't questioned what I knew in my heart to be true. I'm so unspeakably grateful that we made the decision that we did, but I can't help but wish that I'd been stronger. I can't help but wish that when they said "You need to put him in this school. You need to let him go," that I'd had the courage to stand up and announce,

"You know what? As a matter of fact, I don't."

~ Jennifer McGrail

209

24. How Do You Handle an Unschooled Child Asking for a List, a Schedule, or Instructions on What to Do?

My oldest liked to have a general idea of what to expect and would make her own schedules so she knew. I blame myself. When she was small I got into "Managers of Their Homes" and was *all about the schedule*. It stressed us all out. I finally figured out that schedules make me panic and I need to *not do that*.

So instead I keep a general rhythm that changed with the seasons. My husband works from home as a writer and programmer. He needs tons of quiet when he is "in the zone" and tends to have his sleep change with his patterns – if he needs lots of quiet it flips so he is working at night.

As the seasons change I adapt so the kids and I are getting time with him when he is fully functioning and not trying to focus on work. I keep patterns for myself in order to make sure I am getting things done and try to keep things predictable for my oldest. Breakfast, take pills, exercise (in season), cleaning, lunch, downtime, dinner, snack, bed. This gives the kids patterns to work around.

And during seasons where we have lots of outside activities we work around those , keeping mind the time it take sus to get out the door. (A wise friend once told me to add an extra half hour to getting ready per child.) I also have patterns for when we leave the house. When they were small I would only leave the house every other day so we weren't using so much gas.

Nowadays my work helps dictate the schedule. I always work the same days so they know that I work twelve hours on Sunday; am home and having downtime all day Monday; Tuesday I take Grandma shopping and work a twelve-hour overnight; Wednesday I sleep to catch up and work overnight; Thursday I sleep part of the day and then start getting caught up on household stuff; Friday is Sabbath prep; Saturday is Sabbath and no work.

We all work around that schedule naturally, and as it changes we naturally roll with it.

~ Heather Young

———

Before we started fully unschooling, I tried to keep a loose schedule, but I've never been a scheduled person, and I've never really liked to have a schedule. So, my kids have never really craved a schedule. My oldest does like to know what is going to happen next, but we just accomplish that by informing him if something is happening the next day or whatever.

211

I am the type of person who needs to catch up on sleep frequently. Hubby keeps the same sleep schedule most of the time. Very rarely does he sway from that, so on his days off he's often up with the little ones. As far as sleep for the kids, the younger two go to bed at the same time (8pm) but the older two go to bed about the same time we do. If we need to go to something the next morning I just tell them and have them go to bed a bit earlier.

~ Lilly Walsh

———

I *love* lists. The rest of my family not so much. They all realize that at times a list aids in organizing, so they make them as they want them.

We have a large dry-erase calendar that I fill in at the beginning of each month. Each family member has a separate color, so it is easy to see what appointments or activities each of us has each day of the week. We add or erase as changes occur. This fits everyone well as it keeps things organized but for those who do not like creating lists, they never have to since the one who loves to gladly does it for them.

~ Pam Clark

———

I hate lists, so I struggle to meet my kids' organizational requests. They know to make their own lists.

I don't have a single child that wants to be told what to do! They must've got that from their father. No really.

But they do come and ask what they should do with their day, because we've cultivated a habit of all checking in with each other to see what has to happen, what things people have been planning and really wanting to do, etc. We have a flexible framework in our house where we let them know what's upcoming for the following days or weeks as needed. This has started by example between my husband me, as we do the check-in to stay up to speed with each other's goals and commitments.

When they were smaller, for awhile I wrote down that we'd do such-and-such when Daddy was on night shift, such-and-such on day shift, and such-and-such when he was at home, because his shift schedule changes up our household every couple of days. That helped them remember to have quiet time when he's sleeping during the day, which they do automatically now. They quickly learned to trust that they'd have the freedom to get more rambunctious when he's around.

This adaptability is paying off well. Although they tend to sit around in their pajamas till noon if both their parents have been working late (I do my editing work late at night), our oldest has quite successfully held down a seasonal agricultural job with 5 am starts and twelve-hour days.

~ Erica C. Maine

I don't have anyone who asks for a to-do list. I think that it could be because none of them have attended school, the concept just isn't familiar to them. Well no, my oldest attended a schoolish daycare off and on until she was four years old, but she's never been at a loss when it comes to ideas or interest.

I think that if anyone asked for a to-do list, I'd ask why and ask for specifics, a cleaning to do list? A schoolish to-do list? Then I would help them come up with one and it would be up to them to get it done or do something else.

~ Patrice London

_____

My oldest could care less about a schedule or list, so she was glad when we started unschooling. She has asked me a few times about getting "caught up" on math, and she wanted to improve her writing and spelling skills, so we talked about it and I helped her find resources. I asked if she wanted help remembering to use them and for math she said yes. I usually just suggest once in a while when she is wandering around, like, "hey you know you could work on some Khan if you wanted to."

My hubby is much more into schedules and lists and so when he sees my sanity waning he sometimes goes into panic mode and institutes a schedule, which then I am supposed to keep the kids accountable for, and I end up resenting because it is more work for me. We've talked about it; he doesn't understand how I don't like rules and lists because I am a very free-flowing flighty head who hates remembering that kind of stuff. Every chore chart or incentive scheme ever attempted on me lasted a max of two days. So hubby will say that the kids have to be working on a project three mornings a week to give me some quiet time. He expects me to come up with projects and dole out this schedule. I end up just letting the kids pick something from our bookshelf or a topic to study or research during those mornings and it seems to satisfy everyone.

I think a lot of has to do with motivation. I know people that are super-motivated by incentives and schedules. I find that I am more motivated by relationships in my life (not wanting to disappoint when something is due or expected).

My middle daughter does like lists, but she makes her own. She has always unschooled. She will make a list of things she wants to look up, or accomplish in a day. She likes to be notified if some major change of plans or daily routine is coming up.

Now, when I say daily routine, I mean the flow of our house at the time. We kind of have a flow in each season of life. Right now, we stay home most days unless I need to run errands or we have planned a park day or outing (which we have to plan because we use public transportation, walk, etc). Saturdays some or all of us play at the USO. Sundays are family day and Sabbath rest; we might do something fun as a family or stay home and catch up with each other and listen to worship music, sermon, Bible audio, etc.

~ Aadel Bussinger

I'm a list-maker. Schedules stress me out but lists are awesome for me. I make lists for myself, not for my kids. But the kids have picked up on it and do occasionally ask for help with list-making. Usually of the "I have this big thing I want to do and don't know how to make it manageable" variety. So I work with them to break their big project down into bite-size pieces and they list it all out and that's the end of it. It's *their* list and it's up to them what to do with it. I don't mean that in an uncaring way but more in an "I refuse to hold them accountable for their goals" way. For one, once the list is written it tends to vanish but she works through what was on the list from her head. For another, the list usually ends up on a whiteboard somewhere in her room and she crosses things off faithfully. But it's about what suits them, not me. I've never had one ask for a schedule and might have a panic attack if they did because, like I said, schedules cause me tremendous stress.

As far as when they ask to be told what to do, it usually stems from them feeling overwhelmed and looking for help. They don't want me to tell them what to do *per se*, just to help them figure out what to do. Sometimes because they're overwhelmed they may word it awkwardly so I always try to dig in and figure out exactly what they're wanting then I do my best to help them out. But I'm not so good at telling people what to do anyway so it's probably a good thing that's never been what they wanted.

I have one right now that's at a loose end while waiting for a huge download to finish (Steam is awesome for buying and managing games but downloading modern video games on a 3 mbps connection blows chunks). She's mentioned not having anything to do. But she hasn't asked for advice or suggestions and she's filling that "empty" time pretty admirably without my help so I'm leaving it alone.

~ Mariellen Menix

––––––

I think we sometimes get lists and schedules too intertwined. Lists and schedules can go together, but they can also be about very different things. I'm a list maker because I like organization (even though I am not always organized), because I want to remember things and the world is full of too many things for me to remember. Unless your child is either (1) born with a love of

216

list making, or (2) programmed into believing they are important by someone else who likes or relies on them, they might really just not care. So if any of us think we should be concerned about whether or not our kids participate in such things, let it go! If, or when, they find them of interest, they will either run with it on their own, or ask for help in one way or another.

If you as an adult think some form of list making or organizational tools are important, first think about your *why* on that. Is it because it is "the way things should be" or because it fits into something good or helpful in your life that brings something nice into your day?

Then, once you know what your *why* is, and how it would be beneficial to you if that is the case, then look into the bazillion different options out there. Do you need a multipurpose something, or do you simply want a tablet for writing those lists? Do you want to use something for menu planning and shopping lists? Do you want it in paper form, or electronic? What fits you? Your personality? Your ease with technology? Your artistic or no-nonsense bent? What will assist you in being a kinder, more patient person? What will get you all tied up in knots if it doesn't work easily? What will interfere with the lives of those around you? What might help you focus in tidbits so that you have more free time for your children, your spouse? What will get you too focused on what is working best for others and spending time on searching through options better suited for another than for you and the needs of your family? And if it keeps you in a schoolish mindset, step away from the whole darn deal and get in the midst of your kids and use your energy on connecting more with them, in each moment.

~ Pam Clark

I do have a child who wants a routine. He does things like personal care and helping out within our family community in routine fashion. Because of it I try to do some of the same. We don't schedule anything but I make sure that I do certain things in the morning, keep brunch at an expected time of day, etc. It's encouraging to him and I can tell it makes him happy that I accommodate his preferences.

He also likes lists and he will usually think of a handful of things he wants to do the next day, write himself a list on the whiteboard, and work through it. I don't enforce him doing any of it, but I will high five him when he's excited about getting something done.

When he was still finding his own personality he would ask me to make him a list. I would oblige, putting all sorts of stuff on it. Then he'd pick stuff off the list to do. Eventually he just came to the point where he doesn't ask me for ideas any more.

I don't really question how it fits into unschooling anymore because I don't like labeling something as unschooling or not unschooling. If lists are what he likes, then lists are what he uses. He's just the sort of person that likes to face the day with a written plan of action. Even if that plan of action refers to model planes or mud pies, reading or math.

It's my job to encourage him in whatever helps him become a lifelong learner and I'm good with whatever organizational tools he finds useful.

~ Traci Porter

When my kids want a schedule or list, we discuss all the options to figure out exactly what they want and why and how best to achieve it, then I help them do whatever it is they want to do. They are fully aware that this is not something that I am forcing on them, but that I am willing to help by reminding them of their own goals if that is what they want.

~ Carma Paden

My kids have never been to school so I think that affects how they perceive these things.

Some personalities stress over a list being an obligation or being representative of an expectation. My oldest has almost a different anxiety. He stresses when he thinks that unexpected events could happen. I think this is why he likes to make a plan for his day. He likes to know what comes next.

My biggest challenge has been keeping a balance for my other two kids who care nothing about plans.

~ Traci Porter

I think that a schedule, a to-do list, and being told what to do are three very separate and distinct things. None of my four kids have ever asked to be told what to do.

My six-year-old daughter went through a period where she decided she wanted to "do school." I took her very seriously, and asked how I could help make that happen. I printed a bunch of worksheets for her, and I wrote the schedule she dictated to me up on the whiteboard (it went something like: storytime, math, recess, writing, art, recess, etc). She announced to everyone that she was going to do school, and was adamant that we start on time, and switch to the next activity at the proper interval. It lasted for exactly one day. That's the closest any of my kids have come to asking for a schedule, although they've all become accustomed to following the calendar in terms of knowing what's coming up when (park days, play dates, gymnastics, karate, etc).

As for lists, I tend to think you're either a person who likes them, or a person who doesn't. I am a big list fan. Huge. So far, none of my kids have shown any big interest in to-do lists, which is fine, although they've all used one, or asked for help with one, at various times for various reasons.

~ Jennifer McGrail

25. How Do You Unschool Teens?

Mine are 16, 14, and 12. With the younger two I am spending a lot of time being their counselor and coach as they figure out relationships, how the changes in their bodies are affecting them, work through their feelings, etc. Nowadays it is more "stop in and check" rather than having littles around me all the time. I have a lot more time to myself because mine are all introverts but I also spend a lot more time helping them work through their feelings, talking through philosophical questions, historic questions, talking about things instead of telling them things.

The youngest has always been kind of younger than his age, and has always had younger friends. Right now he is going through a maturity growth spurt where he is suddenly struggling gaining maturity and insight at an alarming rate, he is struggling with the whole "changing at a different rate from friends and not sure what to do about it" phase so we spend a lot of time talking through that. He is hovering between child and teen and trying to figure it all out. He spends a lot of his day playing video games with friends (mostly Roblox, Garry's Mod, Minecraft, and other old favorites though currently Borderlands 2, Realm of the Mad God, etc.) He spends time Skyping while he does. He also spends a lot of his time right now watching old favorite TV shows: went through a Sesame Street spurt yesterday, Mythbusters, My Little Pony plus lots of Disney Channel stuff. He still builds a lot; he has out his old toys right now, Matchbox racing has been the current thing, also builds with Lego, Snap Circuits, etc. And when it is warm out spends a lot of his time at my dad's at the pond. Definitely in the "nostalgic" stage. He often comes and checks on us where we are, "you need a hug" and comes in for a brief chat before returning to what he is doing, very similar to how we interact with all three and have as they started needing us less.

My fourteen-year-old spends much of the time drawing, reading, watching anime, plus watching old favorite TV shows. Our relationship is at the "come see what I am drawing; I am really proud of this one" stage. We also spend a lot of time talking about relationships. Learning to observe those them, and picking up from books, movies, and anime, what healthy a relationship look like.

This one is my super-introverted kid, and it's only been in the last few months that we've really begun to see leaving the bedroom as a form of communication, instead of us having to go check in periodically. Nowadays, I often read in the living room, and will find my little deep thinker coming out, ready to have full conversations. It's so it is exciting to get a taste of all the stuff going on in that head! We talk everything: politics, cultural behaviors and sociology, psychology, thought processes, history, books, movies, video games. Lots of analyzing behaviors with that one. There is also working on learning all the different things needed to make a video game. Drawing, designing, storytelling, programming, playing and analyzing a lot of games, the works.

My oldest is the most extroverted and also the one who has looked forward to moving out since she was six. She is independent, self-assured, knows her mind, knows her passions. With her we have hit a place where she needs us even less and it is more helping her work toward her goals for the future and listening as she talks out or shows us something cool she has done.

223

She has applied for her first job. She is also an artist and works hard, drawing daily.

I think talking about goals (when they aren't busy) is key. Being a sounding board, helping sort out interests, sort out where they want to be in five or ten years. For instance, my sixteen-year-old's goal is to be able to move out and live in Texas in two years. Fine. Now let's talk about what needs to happen for that to happen and work towards that. Fourteen-year-old really wants to make a video game, and as a result spends a lot of time talking with my husband and me about the things we can do to help with that goal, and works towards those things. And at this point the big goal of my youngest is getting to the point where he is comfortable leaving the house without me or my husband or another adult (doesn't like going uptown with his siblings.). And we are working on that.

~ Heather Young

———

So my kids are sixteen and nearly fifteen. We started unschooling at the beginning of their teen years. One of the things I've learned in the process is to listen and support without judgment. The world will shoot down their dreams readily enough without my help. So if my daughter says she wants to be president I ask her how I can help her reach that goal rather than telling her all the reasons I don't think she'll ever reach it (or why she shouldn't want to!).

But I also try to drive home to them that this is a life stage of trying on dreams and goals, passions and interests they way they try on clothes. It's okay to explore an interest intensely for a time and then decide that it's not for them or not right now. They can have a goal and choose to cast it aside without meeting it; that doesn't make them "quitters."

~ Mariellen Menix

———

My fourteen-year-old has spent the past year shifting gears from a focus on dance to more involvement in theatre. Now she is extending that to a desire to become involved with cosplay, so she is researching characters and costumes. She has a desire to one day work for Disney at one of the theme parks as a princess or other character. This really fits her well as it incorporates her love of acting, singing, dancing, costuming, makeup artistry, and period and character hairstyles. We will see.

She is also looking into a makeup artistry school in Toronto for her future as well. She would love to work movies, theatre, professional dance companies. So she researches all these things, is back to sewing to increase her skills for costumes, she takes voice lessons, she participates in the local community theatre, she is now learning more dance via online videos since there is not a dance place here that meets her needs. She may take a theatre class at the local high school next year and may audition for a dance choir there as well, as we have no community choirs.

She has gathered some books in her room so she can have a good basic understanding of chemistry, biology, physics to be prepared for what may be needed if she goes to makeup artistry school. She chose a book, *All The Math You Will Ever Need*, to have the basic math she will need as well. Those she will look through as she wishes throughout the next two or three years. She has a dance anatomy book recommended to her by a professional dancer that she utilizes for better understanding her body and mechanics for dance. She is currently seeing a chiropractor and he is really good at giving her basic anatomy lessons that she will be able to utilize as well.

My thirteen-year-old is a gymnast and artist and these are her main focus right now. She spends nine hours in the gym each week out of competition season. She is back into drawing a lot and spends many hours on Minecraft, both in building and creating as well as in admin duties. She is not sure what she wants to do in the future, so she focuses on what she wants and needs in the present which keeps her mainly focused on bettering her body and skills for gymnastics, spending time with friends on and off line, and trying out different art mediums. She is expanding her skills in the kitchen a bit, and looking into what is the best nutrition for an athlete. She is finding she needs to focus on some healthy protein options as she is the one in the family who likes meat the least, yet moves the most.

~ Pam Clark

———

My teens are seventeen and thirteen. I adore having teens. They're so funny: adults one minute, little kids the next. I'm really enjoying this time with them.

My oldest has always wanted to work with small engines, and he's doing just that. A lot of it has been self-taught, but he recently signed up for a two-year-long small engine repair program online. He just recently took – and passed – his first formal test. His current plan is to buy and fix broken weed-wackers, lawn mowers, and such, from Craigslist to fix and sell. He's the more extroverted of my teens, so he's always around, talking, sharing with me, bouncing things off of me.

My younger teen is, like me, a big introvert. He spends his days in his room on his computer. He wants to design video games when he's older, is an excellent guitar player, and is about the most mature and laid-back thirteen-year-old you'd ever hope to meet. Because his default is to spend his day alone (except he's not really alone, as he plays lots of cooperative games with his friends online), I have to make a concerted effort to be sure I'm checking in with him and staying connected.

They have such different personalities and interests, and I'm so glad that unschooling gives them both the opportunity to do exactly what they love.

~ Jennifer McGrail

———

My oldest is thirteen and her siblings are much younger, so I think that makes her both very responsible and yet still young at heart. She has to share a lot with them (room, computer, space) and so I try to make sure to give her lots lots of "me" time where she feels comfortable to ask questions and talk about things away from the younger two. We watch a lot of TV and movies together and discuss things. The other night it was *Footloose* and talking about how the character of Ariel really turned her off because of how she threw herself at guys and had no respect for herself.

Anyways, she is an artist and a gamer. She loves to work with technology and so I try to save up for courses and materials she wants to pursue her art. We talk about what she thinks she will be doing in two, five, or ten years. She really wants to work with animals when we get back to the states and she also wants to be more physical; she loves dancing and is looking into that or maybe martial arts.

She does want to go to college as soon as she is ready. She sees me taking online classes and she doesn't know if she wants a four-year degree as much as she wants to pursue art, graphic design, or maybe a vet tech certificate. So we look at tech and design colleges and she reads veterinarian books (very heavy reads).

She also recently expressed the desire to go out with a friend alone and so we worked through meeting her friend in a designated place, taking the subway, asking and paying for things in Korean, being aware of her surroundings, etc. She has gone out twice with her friend and both times made sure to call to check in and be home at the designated time (she actually came home before the time we agreed on).

One of the things she is worried about with college is math, so we try to find websites and videos to learn bits and pieces here and there. She was working on Khan for a while but got bored so we found another free site that is more like games. I keep track of all her reading, projects, etc. and keep a middle school transcript for our own records and in case she wants to take college courses soon.

~ Aadel Bussinger

———

A lot of these are about independence (and rightly so!) but from the perspective of a teen who unschooled myself, I'd just like to add that parents should be very aware of ways they can help their kid out, especially when it comes to stuff like transcripts and diplomas for older teens. I was told to take care of that myself, since I was in charge of my own education, and despite asking this group for tips I still haven't gotten around to doing it; it's hard and unpleasant and my brain has been 100 percent focused on taking care of myself mentally and physically the past few years, getting myself closer to the life I want. A diploma and transcripts are just not a priority for me, although they weigh on my mind occasionally. That's one area I wanted my parents to help out with, and I'm sure a lot of other unschooled teens would agree, especially those who aren't sure if they want to go to college or not but want to be prepared in case they do end up going. Even teens who *know* what they need to do and how to do it sometimes need help actually doing it. The teen years are a quest for independence, yes, but it's good to keep in mind that teenagers are still young and usually feel stuck somewhere in between child and adult, and knowing they can rely on their parents to take care of stressful "school stuff" for them can be very comforting.

~ Heather Galloway (who started unschooling self as teen)

———

For us, unschooling our teens hasn't brought about any scary, huge changes. We began to have deeper talks about goals – both short-term and long-term – talks about if they want to pursue driving, college, jobs, all stuff of life that naturally become options as they grow old enough.

In regard to those talks, while I do bring them up on my own from time to time, it's important to not to force the discussion – try again another time if a chat isn't forthcoming.

One thing we don't do that many mainstream parents of young adults find shocking is we don't insist they have a job and we don't insist they keep a job that is not working out. Our girl got a job that she realized wasn't for her after one shift – she talked with us and she decided to quit that job the next day. Our kiddos don't pay rent, they don't have to buy food. They do pitch in a little each month on the family cell phone plan by choice, because in doing so, we get better plan we all like and enjoy – one with benefits they couldn't afford on their own.

Yes, they're growing up – rather beautifully and brilliantly, I might add – but we're still their number one supporters and we always have their backs, they've only to ask for help and it will be there every time.

I know it sounds like I'm being overly simple, but it *is* rather simple. Once you're living the unschooling life, it's just that – *life*.

~ Dana Tanaro Britt

———

Heather Galloway, my kids are gradually dealing with questions like that and we spend a lot of time talking about them, coming up with solutions, discussing other possibilities. I can't even imagine them trying to go it alone. It really helps to have a facilitator or mentor and general help as you need it.

~ Heather Young

———

Heather Galloway, what you shared is exactly why parents need to be present and available to their children when unschooling. It should not be hands off. It should be as much or little as the child needs at any given time and situation.

Some people (and I am one of them) are late bloomers in math. My brain was not wired for Algebra until I was thirty. I took it in high school. Again in college. Could not grasp it but so wanted to. Felt so dumb. Accused of not trying hard enough. Over the years I would get it out and try again. At thirty, it suddenly all made sense. I was so relieved. My oldest daughter is the same way. We are good with math but algebra was just out of our reach. I think my fourteen-year-old is the same way. So we do not "do" algebra but read the why behind it, so that understanding of it is there whether we can do it or not. Now at soon-to-be fifty, I would like to pull out a few problems and see if I can still do it. Won't be losing sleep if I can't though.

~ Pam Clark

———

Unschooling teens is easy! Well, I confess I don't know how easy it is to transition to unschooling with teens when they have been traditionally schooled or homeschooled previously – there are likely some relationship issues to deal first with if that is the case – but if you've been radical unschooling for a while, continuing it is a breeze.

But to address the specific question, unschooling teens is simple: find out what they are interested in, and help them figure out how to get there from here.

In the case of my four kids, all unschooled from birth and radically unschooled (grace-based respectful parenting) from very early on, that has meant different things. I encourage them all to think of community college (CC) as a great way to get a piece of "official" paper that would open doors for them later on, but a GED or even a cobbled-together high school diploma would also work. Community college is just that – for the community – and does not require a diploma or GED in order to take classes.

My oldest is on the autism spectrum (Aspergers), and is an artist, so we did a very slow start for her. She stayed at home and worked on her art and writing. She didn't start CC early, and for several semesters she only did a class or two rather than full-time, working into it. She got her AA in Fine Arts and has just transferred to university for her four-year degree. She has a math phobia, so I asked her ahead of time if she wanted to learn the necessary math with me, take a homeschool class, or just take remedial math at CC; she chose to do the remedial class, got an A, then got As in all the college math classes too. (Graduated age 22, with a 4.0 GPA.)

My elder son spent his junior and high school years doing theater and taking acting and improv classes at local studios. He began working first as a student director and then as assistant director with the homeschool theatre group he had been in for years; he's on his fourth year of directing with them. He also got his fingerprint clearance card and started teaching acting in an after-school program for a year, and for two years taught improv and acting workshops at the Free to Be Unschooling Conference. Now he is a courtesy clerk at Whole Foods and still directs in the homeschool theatre group.

He took a handful of CC classes before age eighteen but didn't start full-time until after his birthday. He also chose to do the remedial math class, made an A, and then got As in all his college math classes. He couldn't quite decide what to major in, so he just got an AA in general studies, then also transferred to university where he is now studying film and directing. Lucky me, we were able to make his schedule match nicely with his non-driving older sister's schedule, so he gets her to campus and back without bothering me. ;) (Graduated age 20, 3.8 GPA.)

My #3, another son, is just about to turn seventeen and has followed the most traditional educational path. Despite the fact that my two oldest had no interest in anything mathematical, when he turned twelve, I said to him, "You know, I think you might like math. Math has rules, lots of rules. It always follows the rules, and it never, ever breaks the rules." Then I handed him a Saxon math pre-algebra book I had discovered lurking in my garage in a pile of books someone had gifted to me. He sat down and started paging through it, peering intently at the text. On about page four, he looked up and said to me in a dead-serious voice, "This is the *best book* I have ever read." He started assigning himself homework from the math book, and I showed him Khan Academy, which he again assigned to himself as homework and did quite diligently. If we were going on a field trip or other outing, he would ask where we were going, then he would mull it over for a minute and usually reply, "No, I need to stay and do my math homework." (Weirdo!) He started asking me what jobs were available for math nerds, and we discussed all the engineering jobs out there. One day he came to me and said, "Mom, I just heard about the *coolest* job ever: accountant!" (Seriously. *Weirdo!*)

So this kid wanted to start CC classes full-time, *right now*, at age not-quite-fifteen. I wanted him to ease into it (he's the type to make himself sick from too much stress). We compromised with him taking just the beginner's college success class at CC his first semester, while taking some science and math classes at a local co-op to prepare him for the expectations he would meet on campus. He also took a grammar and writing class that was geared specifically to prep for the CC assessment exam, since he did not want to take remedial English (and being under 18, he would have to wait until 18 to take the remedial class, and he didn't want to wait). He took a few more classes at the co-op and started taking two classes per semester at the CC – his placement test put him into pre-calculus for math! This fall he will turn seventeen, and is doing his first full-time CC semester with no more homeschool co-op classes.

He has recently gotten seriously into music: after years of drums, he is also in lessons for bass guitar, he is teaching himself some piano and guitar, and he has decided that Led Zeppelin was the pinnacle of musical progress. He has started playing in various worship bands at church, and he wants to join a rock band. We discussed ways to turn his hard-science head to good purpose with his music passion, and he decided to get his AA in audio production technologies. He'll graduate CC in a couple of years and be able to transfer to university if he wants, or already have a good path to employment. (Age 16, 20 credit hours, 3.85 GPA.)

My baby girl is my social butterfly and decided to join a co-op of her friends, taught by the moms. They've been meeting together for several years, usually with a science and English/history component. She is there to hang with her friends, but of course also gets the benefit of the classes. Most of the others in the co-op are much more "strict schooly" than we are, but fortunately they are fine that we are not. They just ask at the beginning of the year if I want a grade issued (no, thank you!) and go on from there.

She also started CC classes the earliest: thirteen! Two years ago my oldest daughter wanted to take American sign language and all four kids and I decided to take it together. The boys dropped out after the first semester, but my oldest and youngest daughters and I continued for two years. (She also took a pottery class with her older sister.) We have now completed all the sign language classes available at our closest CC campus, but there is another campus downtown that has a full interpreter certification available – and that's what my now-fifteen-year-old daughter wants to pursue. We are taking this semester off, but in spring I'll be heading back to ASL class with her! If she continues with this interest, she could have her interpreter's license in three or four years; but even if she decides to drop it after a while, she will always be able to list that as a second language on her résumé. She's also considered the possibility of working with autistic children and other jobs where knowing sign language would be a big benefit. This semester she is taking a creative writing class on the CC campus with one of her best friends. (Age 15, 20 credit hours, 4.0 GPA.)

So you see that my pattern is figuring out what my kids are interested in, and finding ways for them to pursue that interest. My artistic and autistic daughter just wants to do art (and in fact we have written our first children's book together and she is illustrating it for publication!). I drove my elder son all over creation for years to be in community theater and take acting classes, and now he is studying film and directing (he has the voice for it, that's for sure). I was aware of my younger son's personality and interests, so even though we had never done any formal math, when it occurred to me that math would probably be a very good match for him, I shared it with him and he surprised even me with his high and persistent interest. When we started taking

ASL classes for fun, I mentioned to my younger daughter that I thought her personality would be well-suited to interpreting, and after thinking about it for almost a year, she decided that she agreed and we are pursuing that road now.

There have been other things along the way, of course. We are quite musical: three kids sing and three kids play multiple instruments. Both my daughters sing with a choir, and both play piano and ukulele and compose music. My theatrical son took voice lessons for a couple of years (no instruments), and my younger son takes drum and bass lessons and is teaching himself other instruments (no voice). My oldest is autistic; my second is dyslexic, dysgraphic, and dyscalculic; and my youngest is ADHD.

The thing is, we just live life together. If I think they might find something interesting or intriguing, I share it without the assumption that they *must* respond according to my expectations, and together we find the best way to achieve the goals they have for themselves.

~ Carma Paden

26. Are Teens too Old to Start Unschooling?

It is definitely not too late. I would start with learning about de-schooling and go from there. Baby steps!

~ Dana Tanaro Britt

You can do it. Many do. The *Teenage Liberation Handbook* is great for older children to read and start to figure out what they really want. Heather Galloway is our resident highschooler who dropped out and chose to self-unschool. Mariellen also started late with her girls. I talked her into unschooling when her girls were in junior high I think? They came straight from public school into unschooling. I think they were fourteen and twelve.

First start reading up on deschooling. Then focus on saying yes more and gradually remove arbitrary limits, rules, and have tos.

~ Heather Young

Easing into it and (especially with the older ones) doing some goal setting may help them transition better. It is okay if their goals change. But going from structure to nothing may make them feel like a fish out of water.

~ Gail Pace

When we first moved fully into unschooling I found that a huge list of things they wanted to do, learn, try, really helped mine.

We don't need it anymore but when we were transitioning it helped them come up with new things to look up or try.

~ Heather Young

I can't stress deschooling enough. It is, in my opinion, the single most important thing you have to do in order to be successful when unschooling older kids.

They're gonna shy away from anything that looks "educational" for a while – maybe a month for each year they did school, which is the average. Maybe a lot longer, like me. Maybe a lot less time than that! Each child is different, and one of your teens might take twice as long as another one of your children to adjust. Just be patient and keep communicating with them, supporting what they *do* want to do. Probably a lot of TV and gaming and internet. That's normal. Even massive amounts of it. You should have seen the Netflix marathons I had when I first started unschooling myself.

~ Heather Galloway

Autodidactism is awesome. My husband and I are both always learning. It is just getting your brain to wrap around all the other ways to learn, not just "textbooks/classroom," not just traditional stuff. I am a former teacher and it took a bit for my brain to wrap around, longer than it would someone who wasn't, and add in the family of teachers behind me and the "have to prove I am a great teacher" thing.

~ Heather Young

My kiddos were eleven and thirteen when Heather Young convinced me that we could give up the public school nonsense and thrive. I discovered that we were already instinctively doing many unschooly things without even knowing the word. We were just ruining it by trying to throw public school into the mix. So we ditched public school and thrive we have done. They're (nearly) fifteen and sixteen now and we're not looking back.

I can't even begin to describe how important deschooling is. In some ways we're still deschooling although I think we're mostly done at this point (except the hubs – he's a slow learner).

The other important thing is to know that you *can* ease into unschooling. You don't *have* to just drop everything at once. I believe Sandra Dodd puts it something like "read a little, try a little, wait a while, watch." I don't know what that will look like in *your* house but it might look like deciding to cut one or two classes from your curriculum in favor of allowing your kids to absorb those things from life or it might look like tossing the curriculum out the window once a week to do something fun or it might look like pitching the curriculum altogether. It might look like saying yes to something the kids want to do instead of "doing school" more often.

For us it looked like twelve weeks of messing about with halfway pretending to do some math and science junk because the hubs wasn't ready to let go all at once, and then he relaxed enough that we just moved on and didn't mess about with school anymore.

Nowadays my kids spend their days in art classes with two different teachers, writing fan fiction with friends on the internet, playing video games (which mostly seem to center around those same fan fictions), reading voraciously, watching things on Netflix (all sorts of things from Doctor Who to documentaries to Dirty Jobs to the Barbie animated series). They've branched into cooking on their own instead of "helping" me (which was mostly me giving directions and them following them). They take long "photo-walks" in the pasture. We play board games and work jigsaw puzzles together. Sometimes we read together. Somebody decides to undertake a project and whoever is interested joins in. Right now we have two projects underway: the younger girl and I are joining a fantasy baseball league (oh the *math* of it, my friends!) and we're all working together on starting a square foot garden. We travel together and visit museums and attend lectures and explore our region and our country.

~ Mariellen Menix

––––––––

What a gift you will be giving your whole family. Start slow. Say yes more. Go on summer break now, and never come off of it. What would your kids like to learn, like to do? What are their interests and passions? Let those things guide you. Options and choices are your friends. Trust and partnership will serve you all well. Read the great info on the links, look through previous posts, ask questions. Try, watch, listen, wait, and enjoy.

~ Pam Clark

27. How Do Unschoolers Prepare for College?

First question: does your teen want to go to college? If so, why? What does he or she want to accomplish by going?

As unschoolers, we want to be careful not to limit our kids by promoting the value of one path over another. The value of college has changed with cost inflation, marketplace evolution, economics, the digital age, and many other factors that may be regional or quality-of-life based.

Second, have they researched the field they are going into (what classes are required for the major)?

Knowing the answer to this will help determine what may be useful in a portfolio or transcript.

Third, have they researched schools and looked at entrance requirements?

Working with the specific requirements of specific institutions is the only realistic college prep there is. High schools differ by region, so the way into a particular institution will differ based on how it handles high school qualifications from outside the immediate region. Many times, those are the paths used to admit homeschoolers because they have a nonstandard transcript compared to their region.

Fourth, will they have the maturity necessary to start and finish school or do they need some time to explore options?

While many young people feel the desire (or even pressure) to acquiesce to their parents' agendas, many also don't have a clear picture of the next five years of their lives. It can be easier for them to give in to others' ideas than to claim the space to formulate their own. But we can hold space for them to develop their dreams in their own way, no strings attached.

How Do Unschoolers Prepare for College Writing and Math?

Writing well is often more related to how much they read. My eleven-year-old hates writing, but is a very good reader and a good speller. As a result, he can write appropriately compared to peers. Writing well in college can be easily learned nowadays because of all the resources available.

Algebra is best learned when mature enough. I struggled with math in high school. In college it became so much easier.

Yes, your teens may have to start off in some remedial classes the first semester. So do many public schoolers who change streams. But because they have chosen this path, self-motivation and having not been in the classroom for thirteen years will work to their advantage. Maturity will keep them committed, because they have learned through unschooling how to seek out their own interests and achieve their own goals.

How Do Unschoolers Prepare for College Through Life and Work?

If I had it to do again, I would have worked to save money and then traveled or joined the Peace Corps. I was raised to believe college was way more important than it actually was.

A final note: after going to school and getting a master's degree, I swore I would never go back to school. Until eleven years later, when I decided to become a nurse after age forty! School can come any time in life. The rush for it to come right after high school causes a lot of people to drop out or finish with a degree that has no real purpose for them and oftentimes with debt.

~ Gail Pace

28. How Do You Handle Transcripts and Diploma or GED?

I have four kids, teens and young adults. All of them started taking community college classes somewhere between the ages of thirteen and seventeen. Two have now graduated with their two-year associate's and have transferred to a four-year university where they'll be going this fall.

All of my kids just started taking the community college classes; none of them had a GED or even high school transcript before enrolling. We didn't pay any attention to state high school standards at all. I told my kids that *some* piece of paper would be a very good thing, and they could choose between a legit high school diploma, a GED, or a two-year associate's degree. They've all chosen the community college route, so we pretty much ignore high school standards.

Most community colleges are that way; they are for anyone, whether they have a diploma or GED or not. The initial tests are for assessment and placement, not entrance or acceptance. In my state, it is automatically considered dual enrollment if the student is under 18, but it's up to you if you want to make sure you are getting the "right" credits for high school (we didn't), or just go for the college degree (we did).

~ Carma Paden

Acting as Academic Translator for Your Unschooler

Step Zero: Let Go of Artificial Educational Ideals

This is not about comparing our kids to the school system's ideals – which, as the daughter of a teacher and a former public-schooled student, I know full well do not get attained in any consistent way.

In fact, that plays out at the post-secondary level too. Out-of-state and international enrollment can be entirely different than attending within your own state or province. Regions tend to stream subjects and the language for them in a unified way, as it facilitates the post-secondary transition. That and tuition breaks for in-state attendance can encourage students to attend locally.

I'm writing this with that in mind. If your young person wants to attend elsewhere, it also may help to have a transcript that reads the way transcripts from your region read. Writing a transcript is like writing a journalistic article or a five-point essay. Knowing the form and content conventions can help it be understood more clearly.

The System Sometime Leaves Kids Behind

When I and my junior high classmates transferred from our tiny local school up to the regional high school, our Grade 10 math teacher had to try to teach us remedial Grade 9 math concepts while maintaining the progress of the overall Grade 10 class, because a particularly poor teacher bombed our Grade 9 studies for us completely.

It all looks good on paper. But in the wild, the idea of prerequisites and acceptable progress is subject to a variety of variables.

The System Sometimes Doesn't Keep Up

On the flip side, my French teacher gave me class credit for reading a novel in French and writing short essays summarizing the content of each chapter. I really wanted to take psychology, which ran in the same time slot. It was only offered in alternate years because of our small school size. To make up the French credit I would have to miss, she accepted me taking a non-credit evening conversational course and demonstrating grammar and comprehension through reading and writing.

Likewise, my high school English teacher recognized that the constraints of her small-town program didn't fully accommodate my creative writing tendencies. She set me up a weekly mentoring appointment with a local poet who lived in the town and gave me permission to go off-campus during my spare.

Teachers do what they can within the constraints they're given. Sometimes the constraint is their own lack of insight or ability, or lack of personal motivation. Sometimes it's the programming limitations. If that's okay in schools, then it's okay for this to happen in homeschools as well. Like teachers, we parents are merely human.

Describing Actual Learning

The advantage we have as unschoolers is, it's not all on us as parents. Our kids, as they become self-directed, fill in the gaps we leave and compensate for what we imperfectly give them. And by being supportive and giving them intellectual and personal freedom, we open the door to true mentorship. Then, according to our own personal strengths, we can fill in gaps for them and help them know they don't have to be perfect either. Someone is there to support them and help work it out.

The goal of transcript writing is to translate that process from our learning environment into the terminology that makes sense to institutions. We want to make our kids' activities understandable to post-secondary institutions that ask for a transcript. In comparing notes on the Christian Unschooling group, we've found that most institutions want the transcript, not the diploma. They want to know what was studied and what percentage of the information was absorbed successfully.

Self-motivated kids (and all people) learn with far greater absorption and retention than when we're put in a compulsory setting and told to take in and regurgitate information in ways that may not even be compatible with our innate learning style – our very brain wiring, let alone our interest, may suffer offense.

Grades and Credit Hours

Rather than seeing grades as a pass/fail or successful/unsuccessful paradigm, I've begun assigning grades based on roughly what ratio of our province's subject matter our kids have covered. It merely shows degree of alignment with provincial curriculum content, not ability to learn or proficiency in acquiring new skills.

I think that's fair. That's all the information public school grading systems provide.

How Are Credits Assigned?

Our regional vocational secondary school only requires approximately 110 hours per credit. Many USA-based homeschool transcript systems use 120 hours of study for a credit. We use the latter as our standard.

This is the equivalent of your child immersing him/herself in a learning experience for eight hours a day, five days a week, for only three weeks. When we allow our students to self-direct and self-regulate their involvement in what interests them, they can achieve major educational goals in a very short time period.

A lot of unschooled kids immerse themselves in one thing, all day, every day, for much longer periods than three weeks. This is similar to the Grade 12 year of a secondary vocational program (say commercial art, for instance) where it's the transition year into college programs. In our province, the senior year vocational program constitutes four credits.

Translating Self-guided Learning into a Transcript

A transcript is a means of communicating information to admissions personnel. The goal in writing it is to understand what's familiar to admissions offices and provide them with the information they need to process an application.

In unschooling terms: it's just a language barrier to hop over. We want to mediate between our children's learning pursuits and commonly used language that summarizes the absorption and retention of recognizable educational content.

The transcript of a child interested in going into a college trades program will look different than that of a kid whose interest lies with a Bible college or seminary program. For instance, I learned in speaking with someone from the local trade school that one of the challenges they experience with accepting homeschool transcripts is, as she put it, credit for ideological studies. (There are a lot of Christian homeschoolers in this province.) Because such studies are outside the provincial programming scope, the college needs further documentation to confirm high school equivalency. Either a GED or a letter from the Manitoba Homeschooling Office confirming satisfactory completion can accomplish that.

Rather than seeing reporting authorities as an enemy, it can be very helpful to build a good working relationship with them where possible. Sometimes (as happens recurrently in Quebec) there's huge antagonism to any form of schooling that doesn't conform to secular public education. Where we have the benefit of positive attitudes in our policymakers, that's something to be glad for. It's an opportunity to build the support system for our kids.

Step 1: What's the "Native Language" Where You Live?

The easiest way I know of for determining your language of translation is to go online. Read school, school board and state/provincial education dept. websites, and determine how they describe the activities of their students.

For instance, I Googled "Manitoba Education curriculum" and got this:

http://www.edu.gov.mb.ca/k12/cur/

But I didn't find the province's vocational information until I thought to search "Manitoba Education Vocational." It's a website design quirk: it isn't linked from the main K-12 page. So it pays to demand the internet tell you exactly what you want to know. :)

Here are the questions I wanted to answer:

- What are the courses called in each grade level?

For instance, consumer math is filed under essential math on the provincial website, but taught as consumer math at the regional high school. Applied math is now the name for the university-entrance stream. It's all changed since I was in high school.

Using the names that the education system uses is helpful. Post-secondary schools will see them on other kids' public school transcripts and know what you're referring to.

- What are the goals and outcomes?

Outcome-based education has taken over my province's schools. OBE curriculum summaries are sort of a soft-core approach to student outcomes, because it's a lot about values formation and placing information in a citizenship context.

However, the style of the descriptions also means that equivalent education (the legal standard I'm required to provide to my kids in this province) is easier to write up. Course descriptions are less in boxes of required information units and more in related out-come streams that incorporate both general information and thinking and behavioural standards.

Because OBE attempts to synthetically engineer well-rounded students, conversationalists, and thinkers, its specific outcomes can be very handy for noting the non-bookwork aspects of our kids' activities.

Here's the Manitoba Framework of Outcomes for Grade 9-12 math:

http://www.edu.gov.mb.ca/k12/cur/math/framework_9-12/index.html

Take a look at the instructional focus, which says that teachers must determine which order of concept presentation works best in their context.

Think of this: If your kid is teaching herself, it's fair for her to make decisions about engaging with concepts based on her learning context. Because she is not wrangling thirty of herself, twenty-five of whom don't even see the point, she'll probably get even farther than a classroom instructor can.

http://www.edu.gov.mb.ca/k12/cur/math/framework_9-12/instruct_focus.pdf

Those of you who have geek or gamer kids will really enjoy the Analyzing Games and Numbers critical thinking group:

http://www.edu.gov.mb.ca/k12/cur/math/framework_9-12/grade12_essential.pdf

Because we as unschoolers want to cultivate young people, not just information, OBE's tendency to evaluate for personal qualities can actually be helpful. Specific outcomes like demonstrates self-directed application of Concept X are kind of a shoo-in.

OBE can be a thorn in the side to curriculum traditionalists, but it gives unschoolers the opportunity to recognize the development of the whole person in their child.

- How many credits constitute a stream of study?

We generally think of the three or four core science, math, and English credits in high school, depending on whether your schools start their credit system in Grade 9 or 10. However, the answer to this delighted me with the provincial trades curricula, because the credit hours are actually reflective of the level of work my son has done.

The four-year stream in our province gives students:

Sampling (Gr. 9) – ½ or 1 credit

Exploration (Gr. 10) – 1 credit

Specialization (Gr. 11) – 3 credits

Transition [into college] (Gr. 12) – 4 credits (http://www.edu.gov.mb.ca/k12/cur/teched/sytep/docs/overview.pdf, page 6)

- How many credits are required for graduation?

Back in my day, it was 20 credits in Grades 10-12. Now, my province requires 30 credits in Gr. 9-12.

Keep in mind, for immersive kids doing self-directed learning, that four-year requirement amounts to around one-and-three-quarter years for all their high school. It sounds daunting because of how we've learned to think of a credit's worth of school programming (long and drawn out), but unschoolers tend to barrel through the time and content when they're in love with a thing.

- What are the actual "compulsory" credits?

I went to a tiny rural high school with almost no program options, so I didn't think of it till we moved to a bigger city: tare different types of high school diploma and they all mean something useful. Not just the three horrible stereotypes I grew up with: the standard diploma, the flunked-the-university-entrance-stream diploma, and the flunking-independent-adulthood (modified) diploma. You can just imagine how that played out for kids whose learning style is hands-on instead of textbook-oriented, and for neuro a-typical kids: not very fair or sensible thinking.

What I learned about vocational curriculum standards removed my worry that my kids would face those stereotypes at the post-secondary level. In reality, our kids just need to be able to clearly explain to others what they've done to cultivate understanding and skills in their area(s) of interest.

Step 2: Don't Alter Reality, Accommodate Reality

Think Outside the Standard Homeschool Box

If your student loves trades, it pays to look into the graduation requirements of your local tech-voc (vo-tech in the US) high schools. I found out that it doesn't matter whether my son did his pre-university sciences (chemistry, physics, biology) at all, let alone in any way that translates into curriculum standards, because the vocational stream replaces them under our province's standards.

The only compulsory credits for Grade 12 in the vocational stream are English language arts and math, which can be a consumer math credit. The vocational program includes trade-specific mathematics – just like we do at our house when we do hands-on vocational work with our kids!

This is very different from some of the crazy competition and self-justifying performance standards I've encountered in textbook and program-based homeschooling circles, where the parental goal is sometimes to rack up and over-attain university entrance book work. Worse, some curriculum sellers and conference presenters seem to exist on scaring parents into that mentality. If kids know they wants to go to university, I can facilitate that path. But as parents we're not messing anything up by letting them branch out into their own explorations.

If it's something that's done in the world – if they can look it up on the internet to find out more – there's probably a commercial aspect to it, which means there's a school somewhere that wants you to buy related knowledge products from them.

In the meantime, there's a good chance your kids are learning online from aspiring student, semipro, or professional content.

Pay Attention to the Extracurricular Angles

In the public schools' thinking, there are some extracurricular credits available some of the time, but the requirements to earn them can create constraints. On the other hand, if it's stuff your kids are already doing, you can credit them for it and know that their transcript will make sense.

Here's an example: music credit is a bit frustrating where I live. Credit is not given for taking private lessons outside the schools. It's only allotted if a kid completes the Royal Conservatory of Toronto's classical exams. Which means that, for instance, bluegrass studies are pretty much out. However, our kids formed a band together, which is a music ensemble. That has also provided them with two major business projects (produce an album and put on a concert) and aligned with some of our provincial requirements for business education credit.

They've also participated in community ensembles of a huge variety, from German polka to classical orchestra to church choir and leading worship. They've had far more involvement than they'd have time for if they were doing extracurriculars around a seven-hour school day. They definitely get music ensemble credit, just like band program or high school orchestra.

As a result, my son's transcript isn't a full reflection of his abilities and commitment to learning. I haven't given my kids credit for individual music studies, even though they've put in hundreds of hours of solo rehearsal time. It could come across as kind of duplicitous to a registrar reading the transcript.

There are a lot of public-schooled kids out there, equally dedicated, who also don't get that recognition. This is a communication document we're writing, intended to convey information in a way that can be clearly received at the far end, so I want the transcript to respect the receiver's context.

Step 3: Keeping Records Through the High School Years

The portfolio is the record of projects and studies. The transcript is the document required for post-secondary admissions. Here's a rule of thumb: portfolio equals making money; transcript equals spending money. Which is something to keep in mind before we panic about a child's disinterest in post-secondary studies.

Portfolio

Portfolio is far more important and flexible than a transcript. It can be used to gain acceptance into hard sciences and university mathematics, to get a job in various design fields, and is a standard item in many arts fields. For example, the Landscape Architects Network has this post discussing how to put professional touches onto a job application portfolio:

http://landarchs.com/designing-your-portfolio/

Portfolio pages can be fairly simple, or they can include design for presentation to colleges and employers.

At our house, portfolio has traditionally been something I do on the side, by observing my kids in action. Until they have a reason to motivate them, it's not going to be super-interesting to them to do it.

- For personal record-keeping purposes, portfolio elements can be things like these: Written or typed work, such as creative writing (called clips in publishing)

- Reading list

- Journal or blog that you or your kid keeps (can be set to private)

  ○ Going back through our own posts to our online homeschooling groups can be really useful for this.

- Photographs of projects

- Jotting down what the kid has mentioned about struggles and triumphs with personal projects (problem-solving skills)

- Jotting down spontaneous discussions that occur

- File of extracurricular certifications such as sports or music achievements

- Art portfolio

- List of business skills

- Non-credit certifications that tie in to credit programs or employment skills

  - Our local college offers several weekend and evening options for learning office and commercial design software.

- FoodSafe certification for restaurant workers, customer relations for retail employees, and other workplace-related continuing education.

The aim of portfolio-keeping is not to torsion our kids into having the "right" conversations or doing the "right" projects so we can record the "right" material. It's to observe and describe what they're already doing.

To create a portfolio, we can attain general familiarity with educational terminology and descriptions, and get in the habit of journaling notes in that language. I can't recommend this for unschoolers, because it takes the approach of putting schoolish thinking ahead of natural activities.

Alternately, we can make our own notes and then go looking for intersections between curricular specifics/terminology and what we observe. That search can take place at the secondary or post-secondary level.

Personally, I prefer the second approach. Instead of shoehorning them into narrow academic preconceptions, it affirms to me that they're excelling in their fields of interest.

Transcript

The transcript is a summary of what may or may not have made it into an unschooler's official portfolio. It provides an overview of the student's educational aims and aptitudes. Unlike the portfolio, its sole purpose for existing is to satisfy educational gatekeepers.

I've found it helpful to start working on the kids' transcripts as they reach the conventional age for accumulating credit hours. Otherwise I'd have a terrible time trying to remember everything they do! Especially with four of them all hitting the teen years fairly close together.

Where the sample transcript is adapted from available standards:

Both home economics and business education are being offered as vocational specializations in Manitoba. However, our business education hasn't covered the full range of the vocational programs, and our home ec isn't precisely equivalent to the provincial specialization diploma either, which exists to feed into the vocation of home economist (http://www.mahe.ca/).

But many schools offer these courses simply as electives under their standard diploma. (For example, see http://www.edu.gov.mb.ca/k12/dl/iso/previews/gr9_home_ec. pdf) Homeschool diplomas are entirely non-accredited in this province, so my only purpose is to summarize my son's range of knowledge and ability.

Step 4: Communicate with Post-Secondary Schools

It behooves me to note that this isn't really the last thing to do. This is all more of a wibblywobbly timey-wimey business than a linear process.

As my homeschool liaison advised, it's a good idea to open the line starting with the beginning year of your local credit system. What the universities and colleges tell you may give important ideas for how to do your portfolio and transcript.

Keeping the Pressure Off

Most kids don't know what they want. When they do, let's face it, they tend to be a lot more annoying. :) That's okay. They don't have to know. We just need to do the parental thing and support them in the present, without placing some hypothetical future above that.

In order to keep the post-secondary idea low pressure, it might help to treat it as a dream factory:

Where would you like to go? What interests you? What do you think is cool?

If a kid is daunted by the whole idea, we as parents can call admissions offices and look into it for our own information, so that we're prepared to meet our kids' needs. We don't have to hold our kids responsible to direct us with premature or uncomfortable decision-making. They may decide not to go with post-secondary education at all. Our job is neither to make the decision for them nor to demand it of them, but to be equipped to facilitate it for them.

My husband's college training is quite technical, and has all been through on-the-job opportunities. His company purchased him the books, and he wrote a series of challenge exams. My own field of choice, book publishing, is very open to freelance port-folio building through work experience. It helps to have mentor-ship and support, but I've learned on my own, by seeking out ex-periences and informational resources.

By my own experience, I can tell you it's perfectly possible to knock a job recruiter's socks off with a portfolio and resume rather than a college diploma.

Assessing Post-Secondary Realities

I suspected after I talked to my son's school of preference that the reality might be very intimidating for him, and might even compromise his love of music if he went for it in a way that doesn't suit his goals and personality. In order to afford an American university, he would have to either conform to the aca-demic performance requirements of scholarships, or come up with alternatives to full-time enrollment.

We also noticed that year 1 involved very little actual music (and yet would still cost him $18,000 in tuition). First-year university programming tends to be designed to level the playing field across a diverse student body. He found that demand offensive to his sense of fiscal responsibility and his desire to focus on music.

Unfortunately, as a non-American it's not possible for him to work while on a student visa, so his choice has been to slow off, make some money, and get himself a backup career to support his real love. Since he doesn't care about earning a degree – he just wants the experience and the networking of a certain music program – we concluded it might be most suitable for him to save up for awhile and eventually audit his choice of courses.

In the meantime, he's looking at the much less expensive option of trade school here in Canada, where he can also continue to work while studying.

Again: portfolio equals making money; transcript equals spending money. It's fair for him to set his goals and priorities accordingly.

In the meantime, my job as a parent is to unschool myself about how to unschool. And hopefully, when my kids witness that process, it'll draw them in and take away any intimidation they might feel about choosing their own future as fully autonomous adults. The best way to make them ready for the adult world is to demonstrate being a grown up.

They'll catch on fast.

~ Erica C. Maine

Appendix A: Definitions

Autodidact: Someone who has learned a subject without the benefit of a teacher or formal education; a self-taught person.

Autonomous education: Education where the student is fully in charge. Includes unschooling and Sudbury/democratic schools.

Charlotte Mason method: Whole child systematic education developed by Charlotte Mason. "Education is an Atmosphere, a Discipline, a Life."

Child-led learning: Education programs in which children are responsible for deciding what to learn.

Classical education: A specific three-part process for training the mind. The early years of school are spent in absorbing facts. In the middle grades, students learn to think through arguments. In the high school years, they learn to express themselves. This classical pattern is called the trivium.

Curriculum: A specific course of study, usually a collection of materials.

Cyber school (virtual school): An online school. Students are taught primarily online. Very often connected to a public or private school.

Democratic schools: Alternative schools where the children have equal say in their lives as the teachers.

Deschooling: The period of time between choosing to leave traditional education methods behind and the paradigm shift where the brain stops thinking about school as the only form of education. Takes at least 1 month per time spent in school.

Gentle parenting: Also called grace-based, positive, or peaceful parenting; an extension of attachment parenting. Moves away from authoritarian parenting with a focus on connection, relationship, and mutual respect.

Homeschooling: Parents educating their children at home (or in the world instead of school).

Interest-led learning: Sometimes called inquiry-based learning. Focused on studies following interests instead of a set curriculum.

Non-aggression principle (NAP): An ethical stance that asserts that aggression is inherently wrong, where aggression is defined as initiating or threatening forcible interference with another's person or property.

Montessori: A scientific child-centered educational approach developed by Maria Montessori. The child is viewed as naturally eager for knowledge and capable of initiating learning in a supportive, thoughtfully prepared learning environment. It attempts to develop children physically, socially, emotionally and cognitively through a specific scientific method.

Radical unschooling: Gentle parenting combined with unschooling. Sometimes called whole-life unschooling.

Self-directed learning: Student guided learning; can be more or less structured.

Sudbury school: Type of democratic school.

Strewing: Deliberately leaving items of interest in the path of children.

Umbrella school: A government-recognized entity that acts as a go-between for parents and government. Sometimes acts as a private school over homeschooling parents.

Unparenting: A hands-off or laissez-faire style of parenting with little or no discipline. (Note that elsewhere this may be defined differently, but this is the meaning for the purposes of this book.)

Unschooling: An educational method focused on allowing the child and family the freedom to follow their interests wherever they go and whenever they change; term coined in the 1970s by educator John Holt.

Waldorf method: Education method based on the work of Rudolf Steiner emphasizing the role of imagination in learning and strives to integrate the intellectual, practical, and artistic development of pupils in a holistic manner. The goal is to develop free, morally responsible, and integrated individuals equipped with a high degree of social competence.

World schooling: Travel based homeschooling; many possible styles, depending on the family.

Appendix B: More Resources

Research journals dedicated to unschooling research:

Journal of Unschooling and Alternative Education by Nipissing University, Canada

https://jual.nipissingu.ca

Educational Researchers (for those who want to know how children learn and the research that backs up the unschooling principles):

Alison Gopnik http://alisongopnik.com/

- The Gardener and the Carpenter https://amzn.to/2LBjzyz

- The Scientist In The Crib https://amzn.to/2JReqNJ

- The Philosophical Baby https://amzn.to/2LM17BE

- How Babies Think https://amzn.to/2uLGf5p

Peter Gray
https://www.psychologytoday.com/us/experts/peter-gray-phd

- Free to Learn https://amzn.to/2JQ0xzj

John Holt https://www.johnholtgws.com

- How Children Learn https://amzn.to/2LuQ5lZ

- How Children Fail https://amzn.to/2JNcF49

- Teach Your Own https://amzn.to/2A6mevE

- Learning All the Time https://amzn.to/2LwVVmH

- Instead of Education https://amzn.to/2LkOyzG

- Never too Late https://amzn.to/2uRYzKv

- Growing without Schooling https://amzn.to/2LBAuAW

Alfie Kohn https://www.alfiekohn.org/

- Unconditional Parenting https://amzn.to/2uO3EDf

- Punished by Rewards https://amzn.to/2LkQ9pa

- What Does It Mean to Be Well Educated? https://amzn.to/2JMHjLb

- The Whole-Brain Child https://amzn.to/2A6QAhn

- Beyond Discipline https://amzn.to/2NImuTr

- The Myth of the Spoiled Child https://amzn.to/2Oen7Fy

- Feel-Bad Education https://amzn.to/2Livl1s

Harriet Pattison and Alan Thomas
http://www.educationalhereticspress.com/titles-rethinking-learning-to-read.htm

- Rethinking Learning to Read https://amzn.to/2LKwxGY

- How Children Learn at Home http://amzn.to/XjkWTu

———

Educators who write about unschooling:

John Taylor Gatto http://Johntaylorgatto.com

- Underground History of American Education https://amzn.to/2mE7r1u

- Dumbing Us Down https://amzn.to/2A8X2Vi

- Weapons of Mass Instruction https://amzn.to/2LlKj6G

- A Different Kind of Teacher https://amzn.to/2NIKS7h

- The Exhausted School https://amzn.to/2NGuUdQ

Pat Farenga http://patfarenga.squarespace.com/

- Teach Your Own with John Holt https://amzn.to/2LnPPWM

Clark Aldrich http://unschoolingrules.blogspot.com/

- Unschooling Ruleshttps://amzn.to/2LleivJ

Unschooling families who write about unschooling:

Blake Boles

- Better than College https://amzn.to/2OhVxXT

Joyce Fetterol https://www.joyfullyrejoycing.com/
Pam Laricchia https://livingjoyfully.ca/

- Free to Learn with Unschooling 3 book series https://amzn.to/2A8Wn6g

- What is unschooling? https://amzn.to/2LKRd1z

- Unschooling: A field guide https://amzn.to/2LjptVG

Grace Llewellyn

- Teenage Liberation Handbook https://amzn.to/2A4wOTI

- Guerrilla Learning https://amzn.to/2uLJvOt

- Real Lives https://amzn.to/2mEeA23

Mary Griffith

- The Unschooling Handbook https://amzn.to/2NSez6i

Books that would be beneficial to all homeschooling parents:

Lori Pickert

- Project Based Homeschooling https://amzn.to/2NIsnQx

Lenore Skenazy https://letgrow.org/

- "Free Range Kids" https://amzn.to/2A84CiT

Tammy Takahashi

- Deschooling Gently https://amzn.to/2LF8pbV

Shamus Young

- How I Learned https://amzn.to/2LrWzma

Gentle Parenting books

LR Knost http://www.littleheartsbooks.com/

- Jesus, the Gentle Parent https://amzn.to/2uMZzPU

- Two Thousand Kisses a Day https://amzn.to/2LmRlIJ

- Whispers Through Time https://amzn.to/2JRTpm2

- Gentle Parenting Workshop 1 https://amzn.to/2Li4W3M

- Gentle Parenting Workshop 2 https://amzn.to/2LiR3CD

Jessica Bowman

- Parenting Wild Things: Embracing The Rumpus https://amzn.to/2uS9bZM

Meet the authors

Jessica Bowman

Mother of 4 wild things, ages 17, 14, 12, and 10, owner of Psychedelic Doilies (https://psychedelicdoilies.com/) and author of Parenting Wild Things (amazon.com/author/jessicabowman)

Dana Tanaro Britt

Author (https://www.amazon.com/-/e/B00YEQOP48), wife, mother of 2 radically unschooled now-adult children (current ages 23 and 25), devout pizza appreciator, inspired by everyday life where ordinary people are making happily ever after happen one moment at a time.

Karen Bieman

Karen lives in Australia and has 4 children aged 15, 18, 22 and 24. She came to unschooling when one of her children was struggling to adjust from a small community school in the outback, to a large public school in the city. What started as a 12 month solution, back in 2005, became a way of life that is still continuing. Unschooling has enabled her children to thrive and pursue their varied passions, from surfing, circus and theatre, right through to social justice and working with refugees. Karen is herself excited to be finally pursuing her own almost-lifelong dream to become a counsellor. You can find her at www.karenbieman.com - She also writes about unschooling and parenting at https://www.facebook.com/ConnectionParenting/ and is a founder of the Facebook group for Australian unschoolers:

-
Karen has travelled much further along the unschooling path
than when she wrote the musings in this book and dreams of
writing more in the future!

Aadel Bussinger

Former unschooling mom, now super awesome high school
teacher. Mom of 3, ages 17, 12, and 7.

Pam Clark

Longtime radical unschooling mom and advocate. A mine/ours/
theirs blended family of 6 kids ages 29, 28, 27, 19, 17, 6.

Sarah Clark

British home educating mum of five, (14, 11, 9, 6, and 9
months.)

Joan Concilio

Joan came to unschooling with her daughter, Sarah, around the
time Sarah was 10 or 11, and they kept on rolling right through
high school graduation in 2018. Joan and Sarah both had eclectic
educational backgrounds before that time, and for Sarah, the
public school system wasn't working at all. When they began
homeschooling, they'd actually already gone pretty far down the
deschooling path, and unschooling came naturally as "the thing
that was the farthest away from what wasn't working." Now that
Sarah has graduated, they continue to live and learn together and
to share their experiences with unschooling, especially through
the teen years. (Yes, you can get a diploma, hold a job, go to college, etc., as an unschooler - as you've surely read through this

book!) Joan and Sarah share their family's story at Unschool Rules (https://unschoolrules.com).

Heather Galloway

Heather came to unschooling as a teen choosing to drop of school as a teen and unschool instead. Heather's primary focus in the community is to bridge the gap between new unschooling parents and their children.

Jessie Lynn

Jessie and Andre' have been married for over two and a half decades and have six children (ages 26, 21,20, 20, 18, and 16) and have been homeschooling for 20 years. We began as traditional homeschoolers with curriculum in a box and all the tears! We learned about the literature approach and delved into that for several years. Unschooling was intriguing but terrifying so we continued to plow through curriculum but our oldest fought me every single day of his high school career. After he graduated in 2010, we realized that he did not know how to manage his day without outside input- that was the final push we needed to embrace unschooling, we wanted the other children to know how to fill their hours without moms schedule. Our children have thrived in unschooling and we have graduated all but the youngest who will graduate in spring of 2019. Preston is a musician and graphic designer (and a husband and dad!), Catherine is a (not-yet-published) poet and novelist who is finishing up her English degree and will likely get her masters so she can be a librarian, Cuyler and Cade are both working full time and learning to be a chef, Skylar graduated from AVEDA and is a licensed Cosmetologist, Geoffrey is pursuing modeling and loves fashion - we can't wait to see where he ends up! Jessie tutors homeschool students in history and government and is the Louisiana State Coordinator for TeenPact Leadership Schools. www.teenpact.com/louisiana.

Patrice London

Patrice is a mother of 5, ages 20, 15, 11, 4, and 1. She is co-owner of Eden's Pure Herbals (https://edenspureherbals.com/) with her oldest daughter. She has radically unschooled her children almost their entire lives.

Stacie Mahoe

Stacie is sports mentor and writer (http://thinklikeachamp.com/) as well as a mom of 8 active kids (current ages 21, 18, 17, 13, 10, 8, 6, and 3) who lives in Hawaii. She came to unschooling after seeing her son struggle in school and hearing teachers say, "he's falling further and further behind in reading year after year" despite the extra tutoring they gave him. School clearly wasn't working for him and that prompted Stacie to take a much closer look into unschooling. She had come across it years prior, and was quite intrigued, but couldn't find the answers to the exact kinds of concerns addressed in this book. Thankfully, this time around, with the support and knowledge of experienced unschoolers who had the courage to share their stories (many of whom are in this book!), Stacie was able to dive in with confidence and now enjoys seeing her children learn and grow like never before!

Erica C. Maine

A grown unschooler (ignoring that very unhappy time in public high school), natural autodidactic, and Canadian mom of 4 rambunctious unschooled almost grown-ups (3 of which have flown the coop). Current ages 22, 20, 18, and 16.

T. McCloskey

Radical unschooling mom to four sons, two of whom are special needs (24, 19, 18, and 12), advocate for children's rights as humans to be raised peacefully."

Jennifer McGrail

Writer at https://www.jennifermcgrail.com/ where she bravely takes on all the hard topics. Mother of 4, current ages 21, 18, 14, and 10, all radically unschooled.

Bay Menix

Homeschooled from the day her mom decided to never ever send her to school ever. Started unschooling at age 8, now a married adult of 20 working on embarking on her own writing and art career and continuing life as a serious autodidact.

Mariellen Menix

Started unschooling her kids when they were teens, due to their unfortunate middle school experiences. Quickly found her kids blossoming in this new educational experience. The kids are now 19 and 20.

Rachel Miller

Married 19 years. 2 kids ages 13 (14 in Nov, so depending on print date) and 15.

Admin on the Christian Radical Uunschoolers Facebook page and Texas Unschoolers. Coordinator for Texas Unschoolers conference. Have been a speaker for Texas Unschoolers and Free To Be conferences as well as guest presenter for Sue Patterson/Unschooling Mom2Mom coaching.

Carma Paden

Carma has four always-unschooled children, ages 22, 20, 16, and 14, and has been married to their dad for over 30 years. After ten years of marriage and acquiring a degree for which she never had a career (elementary education) and a career for which she never had a degree (editor in a very minor publishing house), she promoted herself to being a stay-at-home mom. The intense disaffection she developed for the educational system in her final year of teacher's ed led her directly to John Holt and the firm decision to homeschool her future children. After homebirthing, babywearing, co-sleeping, and breastfeeding four kids nonstop for twelve years, radical unschooling just didn't seem like a very big stretch, so she did that too.

Among her four offspring she numbers one Aspie, one dyslexic, one ADHD, one synesthete, one thespian, one colorblind, one total and complete math nerd, one drummer, two ukulelists, two artists, three singers, and four wildly differing personalities. Plus a cat. Two are in college full-time and two are in community college part-time. But not the cat.

Gail Pace

Gail came to unschooling when she realized her homeschooled first-grade son loved to learn but hated to be told what to learn and how to learn it. She has had a passion for education since high school and experienced a complete paradigm shift while exploring Unschooling in her son's first year of homeschooling. Unschooling has also given her the time and space to pursue her own goals by returning to school as a nursing student. Unschooling has made moving multiple times a lot easier, and her husband is able to spend time with the kids around his crazy work schedule. Gail is also a CU admin. She has two children, ages 12 and 7.

Traci Porter

Traci has 5 kidlets, currently 4mo, 3yr, 8yr, 10yr, and 13yr. They keep her busy with orchestra, sports, robotics, woodworking, art, dance, and countless others.

Amanda Rodgers

Amanda was a public school student for all but her 8th grade school year, during which time her father took her out of the school system and let her learn what she wanted at home. When she started having her own kids, she learned about unschooling in large part from her sister, Heather Galloway, and, realizing that was what she'd experienced for that one glorious school year, she decided to unschool her own children. She and her husband Matthew currently have six kids, ages 12, 10, 8, 5, 2, and newborn.

Heather Young

Artist and illustrator (http://tinybookdragonart.com), author (https://amzn.to/2KHsnhZ), web designer, owner of http://Christianunschooling.com, nanny, tutor, wife of Shamus Young (http://Shamusyoung.com), mother of 3 grown radically unschooled children, ages 20, 18, and 16. Two of which have successfully moved out and moved on with the rest of their lives, all of which continue their autodidactic ways.

Lilly Walsh

Former unschooling mom, in the process of going back to school herself, with 4 kids ages 12, 10, 8, and 6.

Made in the USA
San Bernardino, CA
16 November 2019

59992780R00173